SENSATIONAL
Barbecues

INDEX

CONTE

Olive Damper, page 103.

Barbecued Lobster Tail with Avocado Sauce, page 71.

Thai Chicken Cutlets, page 48.

Orange and Ginger Glazed Ham, page 92.

N T S

Pork Sausage Burger with Mustard Cream, page 29.

Corn on the Cob with Tomato Relish, page 83.

The Publisher thanks the following for their assistance in the photography for this book: Antico's Fruit World; The Bay Tree; Barbara's Storehouse; Barbeques Galore; Corso de' Fiori; Doug Piper's Butchery; Home and Garden on the Mall; HAG Imports; Pacific East India Company; Primex Products Pty Ltd; Potters Agencies.

Mango Upside-down Cake; page 110.

Leg of Lamb with Vegetables, page 98.

All recipes in this book have been double-tested.

When we test our recipes, we rate them for ease of preparation. The following cookery ratings are on the recipes in this book, making them easy to use and understand.

A single Cooking with Confidence symbol indicates a recipe that is simple and generally quick to make – perfect for beginners.

Two symbols indicate the need for just a little more care and a little more time.

Three symbols indicate special dishes that need more investment in time, care and patience—but the results are worth it.

NOTES
International conversions and a glossary explaining unfamiliar terms can be found on page 112. Cooking times may vary slightly depending on the individual oven. We suggest you check the manufacturer's instructions to ensure proper temperature control.

Barbecue Basics

Some barbecues can be as formal as a dinner party, others as
relaxed as a picnic on the beach. Whatever the case, you will need
to be prepared – choose the barbecue that suits you best, light the perfect
fire and prepare the food to its maximum advantage.

Types of barbecues

Fuel-burning

Fixed barbecue Many gardens contain some sort of fixture for barbecuing; they are relatively simple constructions, usually made from bricks or cement and featuring two grills – the bottom for building the fire, the top for cooking the food. These grills are not generally height-adjustable, so cooking can only be regulated by adjusting the fire, or moving the food away from or towards the fire. Being fixed these barbecues cannot, of course, be put out of high winds or moved to shelter in the event of rain. Despite this, fixed barbecues are easy to use and maintain, and quite often are large enough to cater for big gatherings.

Weber (Kettle) barbecue One of the most popular styles of portable barbecue, the weber features a close-fitting lid and air vents at top and bottom which allow for greater versatility and accuracy in cooking. Webers can function either as a traditional barbecue, as an oven or as a smoker (see panel on page 7 for preparation techniques). Weber barbecues only burn charcoal or heat beads (wood is not recommended) and are relatively small. The standard diameter is 57 cm, so if barbecuing for large groups more than one weber is probably required.

Brazier This is the simplest style of fuel-burning barbecue, of which the small, cast iron hibachi is probably best known. A brazier consists of a shallow fire-box for burning fuel with a grill on top. Some grills are height adjustable or can rotate. Braziers are best fitted with a heat-reflecting hood, so that food will cook at an even temperature.

Gas or Electric Barbecues

Although often more expensive, these barbecues are very simple to use. They do not require an open flame, only connection to their heat source. In most cases, the gas or electricity heats a tray of reusable volcanic rock. Hickory chips can be placed over the rock-bed to produce a smoky flavour in the food, if desired. Sizes of models vary, the largest being the wagon style, which usually features a workbench, reflecting hood and, often, a bottom shelf for storage. While small portable gas models, which require only the connection of a gas bottle, are greatly manouvrable, electric models are, of course, confined to areas where mains electricity is available. Most gas or electric barbecues have temperature controls; their accuracy is their primary advantage. Electric models can be fitted with rotisseries or spit turners for spit roasting.

The fire

Fuel

Although traditional, wood is not an ideal fuel for cooking. It can be difficult to light and burns with a flame. Charcoal or heat beads are preferable. They will create a bed of glowing heat which is perfect for

A weber barbecue, although compact, can prepare a variety of foods.

cooking. They do not smell, smoke or flare and are readily available in supermarkets or hardware shops. (Heat beads are sometimes known as barbecue briquettes and should not be confused with heating briquettes, which are not suitable for cooking.)

Firelighters are essential for lighting charcoal or heat bead fires. They are soaked in kerosene so will ignite instantly. Do not attempt to cook while firelighters are still burning, as they give off kerosene fumes.

A gas-fuelled wagon barbecue featuring hood and work areas.

Generally one or two firelighters will inflame about twenty pieces of charcoal or heat beads.

A 'normal' fire consists of about 50–60 heat beads or pieces of charcoal and will last for several hours. All recipes in this book can be cooked over a normal fire.

Preparation

Once lit, fires should be left to burn for about 40–50 minutes before cooking. Heat beads or charcoal will become pale and develop a fine, ash coating when they are ready to use. (Wood will have a low flame and have begun to char.) If preparing a weber (kettle) barbecue, leave off the lid while the fire is developing.

Build the fire in the middle of the grate, so that cooked food can be moved to the edge of the grill and kept warm.

Temperature control

A fire's temperature can be lowered by damping down with a spray of water. (A trigger-style plastic spray-bottle is ideal.) Damping also produces steam which puts moisture back in the food.

The best and safest way to increase the heat of a fire is to add more fuel and wait for the fire to develop. Do not fan a fire to increase its heat; this will only produce a flame. Never pour flammable liquids on a fire.

Coals ready for cooking: Beads have developed a fine ash coating.

Cooking techniques

Most recipes in this book call for the food to be cooked over a direct flame. Recipes using indirect cooking are in Chapter 8. Indirect cooking is only possible on weber (kettle) barbecues. (See panel on page 7 for how to prepare a barbecue for indirect cooking.)

Direct Cooking

As with grilling or frying in the kitchen, the less turning or handling of the food the better. Once the fire is ready, lightly brush the grill or flat-plate with oil. Place the food over the hottest part of the fire and sear quickly on both sides; this retains moisture. Once seared move the food to a cooler part of the grill or flat-plate to cook for a few more minutes. Barbecuing is a fast-cooking process so even well-done food will not take very long. Techniques such as stir-frying are ideal for the barbecue flatplate.

Test meat for doneness by firmly pressing it with tongs or the flat edge of a knife. Meat that is ready to serve should 'give' slightly but not resist pressure too easily. At first, the degree of doneness may be difficult to judge, but try to resist cutting or stabbing the meat; this not only reduces its succulence, but releases juices which may cause the fire to flare. Pork and chicken should not be served rare, so if in any doubt as to doneness remove to a separate plate and make a slight cut in the thickest part of the meat. If the juices do not run clear, return to the heat for further cooking. Test fish for doneness

Retain moistness in the meat by searing quickly and turning once only.

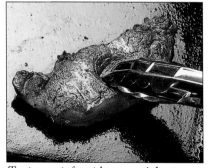

Test meat for 'doneness' by pressing gently with tongs.

by gently flaking back the flesh in the thickest part with a fork. Cooked flesh should be white and opaque, but still moist.

Smoking

Smoking chips or chunks come from hickory wood, mesquite, dried mallee root, red-gum or acacia trees and are available from barbecue specialists and some hardware or variety stores. Their smoke provides an extra and unusual flavour to the food.

Smoking is best done on a covered barbecue (see panel on page 7 for technique) but can also be done on an open fire. Scatter smoking wood throughout the coals. Once the wood is burning, damp down with a little water to create more smoke. Smoking wood is available in chips and chunks; chips burn quickly so should be added towards the end of the cooking process. Chunks should last through the entire cooking process.

If glazing meat, such as ham, and smoking together, always glaze before adding wood. (Please note that some woods, such as pine, cedar or eucalyptus produce acrid smoke and are unsuitable for cooking. Use only wood sold specifically for smoking.)

A barbecue flatplate can be used to stir-fry vegetables.

Fish is ready when the flesh has turned opaque and flakes back easily.

Rare, Medium or Well-Done?

Not everybody likes their steak, beef or lamb cooked for the same length of time. Test for 'doneness' by gently pressing the meat with tongs or a flat-bladed knife. If in doubt, remove it from the barbecue and make a small cut in the meat to check its colour.

Here is a guide to how the 5 classic degrees of 'doneness' should feel and look.

Medium-rare: Springy to touch, with moist, pale-red centre.

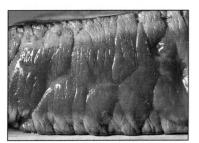

Bleu: Very soft to touch, red-raw inside, outer edge lightly cooked.

Medium: Firm to touch, pink in centre and crisp, brown edges.

Rare: Soft to touch, red centre, thin edge of cooked meat.

Well-done: Very firm to touch, brown outside and evenly cooked.

Flavoured Butters

These butters add an interesting finishing touch to a meal and can be used instead of sauce. They are delicious on beef, pork, lamb, chicken, seafood and fish, as well as cooked vegetables or spread over hot bread.

Make 2 or 3 butters at a time and store, covered, in the refrigerator for up to 2 weeks. Butters can also be frozen and stored for several months. Shape butters into a log and simply slice off the required quantity, then return it to the refrigerator.

Alternatively, place butter in a piping bag and pipe individual servings over a piece of aluminium foil. Store, in refrigerator until required; place on food just before serving. Different flavoured butters can also be served in their own individual pots.

Always soften butter to room temperature before preparing.

Garlic and Cheese Butter

Beat 100 g butter and 100 g softened cream cheese until light and creamy. Add 1 crushed garlic clove and 1 tablespoon each chopped fresh basil and chopped fresh parsley. Beat until smooth. Using plastic wrap, form into a log shape and refrigerate.

Lime and Chilli Butter

Beat 125 g butter until light and creamy. Add 1 tablespoon lime juice, 1 teaspoon grated lime rind, 1 teaspoon chopped chilli and 2 teaspoons chopped fresh coriander. Beat until smooth. Using plastic wrap, form into a log shape and refrigerate.

Savoury Anchovy Butter

Combine 200 g butter, 4 drained anchovy fillets, 2 chopped spring onions, 1 garlic clove and 1 tablespoon grated lemon rind in food processor bowl. Process 20–30 seconds or until mixture forms a smooth paste. Transfer to small serving pots and refrigerate.

Capsicum and Tomato Butter

Cut 1 large red capsicum in half; remove seeds and membrane. Brush skin with oil. Place under preheated grill 5–10 minutes or until skin blackens. Cover with damp cloth and stand 5 minutes. Remove skin from capsicum; discard. Chop flesh roughly. Combine capsicum, 200 g

Shape flavoured butter into a log, freeze and slice rounds as required.

A piping bag and a variety of nozzles can make interesting shapes.

Serving pots can be stored in the refrigerator for several weeks.

chopped butter, 4 drained sun-dried tomatoes in oil and salt and pepper, to taste, in food processor bowl. Process 20–30 seconds or until smooth. Transfer to a serving bowl, cover in plastic wrap, and refrigerate.

Marinating and basting

Because food is cooked quickly on the barbecue, some foods should be marinated beforehand. Marinate food, preferably overnight, but at least a few hours ahead in a non-metal dish, covered, in the refrigerator; turn meat in marinade occasionally. Vinegar, citrus juice or wine-based marinades break down and tenderise the fibres of the meat, and are ideal for tougher meats.

Oil-based marinades moisturise meats and are suitable for meat such as chicken or pork. Yoghurt-based marinades are used with chicken or lamb, generally. The marinade will form a delicious crust over the meat when it is cooked. (See page 14 for marinade recipes.)

Drain food from marinade and cook food as quickly as possible. If marinade is oil- or vinegar-based, reserve and use to baste.

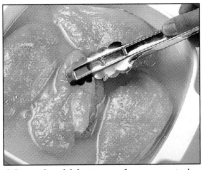

Meat should be turned once or twice during the marinating process.

Basting While not all foods need to be marinated before barbecuing, all should be basted during cooking. Basting seals moisture and prevents the food from sticking. Baste with olive oil or reserved marinade, lightly, on both sides. A pastry brush, or clean, unused paintbrush is ideal for this. Do not use a brush with plastic bristles as the plastic may melt onto the food.

Planning your barbecue

Design your menu to take full advantage of the barbecue – vegetables, kebabs, breads, even desserts can be cooked or warmed easily.

Serve at least 1 salad with the cooked food. Salad dressings and special sauces can be made in advance and stored in a screw-top jar in the refrigerator. (See page 15 for salad dressing recipes.) Assemble salads up to 1 day in advance, but dress just before serving.

Light the fire about an hour before you are planning to use it; check the fire occasionally; it can easily go out if unattended.

Assemble all necessary utensils and accessories – for example, tongs, forks, knives, plates and basting brushes, before cooking.

Have plenty of snacks and drinks available for your guests, but place them well away from the fire.

Have a hose or water bottle standing by in case of emergencies. (As a general safety rule, do not attempt to barbecue in strong winds.) A torch may be useful if barbecuing at night.

Always extinguish a fire once you have finished cooking on it. If possible, clean out the barbecue as soon as it has cooled down; brush or scrape grills and flatplates, discard ash and embers.

Indirect cooking

Indirect cooking roasts or bakes food more slowly than direct cooking. It also allows for adding fragrant wood chips to the coals which introduces extra flavour to the food.

To prepare a weber for **indirect cooking:**
1. Remove lid; open bottom vent.
2. Position bottom grill inside bowl and attach charcoal rails. Heap coals in rails and position firelighters inside coals.
3. Light fire and allow coals to develop to fine-ash stage. (Leave lid off while fire develops.) Place a drip-tray or baking dish on bottom grill. Position top grill; add food.

To prepare a weber for **smoking:**
1. Prepare barbecue as above.
2. When coals reach fine-ash stage, add wood chips; fill drip tray or baking dish with 4 cups hot water. Cover with lid until fragrant smoke develops.
3. Remove lid; centre food on top grill. Cover with lid.

Position two or three firelighters within the coals.

Light fire and allow the coals to develop.

Place a drip tray underneath top grill when coals are ready.

Spoon a generous quantity of smoking wood over hot coals.

NO-EFFORT EXTRAS

Hot Breads

GARLIC BREAD

Cut a French loaf into thick diagonal slices three-quarters of the way through. Combine 125 g softened butter, 2–3 cloves crushed garlic, 1 tablespoon finely chopped parsley and pepper, to taste, in small bowl. Beat until smooth. Spread mixture between each slice of bread. Wrap bread in foil and place on baking tray. Bake in moderate oven 180°C 10–15 minutes or until butter has melted and bread is hot.

Alternatively, place bread on hot barbecue grill or flatplate, turning occasionally to ensure even cooking.

BACON AND CHEESE BREAD

Combine 1/2 cup grated cheddar cheese, 2 tablespoons grated parmesan cheese, 1 finely sliced spring onion, 2 finely chopped bacon rashers and pepper, to taste, in a small bowl. Across the top of a Vienna loaf, at 2 cm intervals, cut diagonal slits 1 cm deep in one direction. Make similar slits in the opposite direction crossing over the first cuts, forming a diamond pattern. Place bread on a foil-lined baking tray. Sprinkle cheese and bacon mixture over the top. Bake loaf in a preheated moderate 180°C oven 10–15 minutes or until cheese has melted and bacon is crisp. Cut into slices with a sharp serrated knife. Serve hot with butter.

TOMATO AND OLIVE BREAD

Cut a French bread stick into 2 cm thick slices using a sharp serrated knife. Spread each slice with a small amount of green or black olive paste. Thinly slice 2 tomatoes. Place 1 or 2 slices of tomato on each slice of bread. Top with thinly sliced mozzarella or bocconcini (fresh mozzarella). Sprinkle with pepper and 2–3 tablespoons finely shredded basil leaves. Place on foil-lined baking tray. Bake in preheated moderate 180°C oven 10–15 minutes or until cheese has melted and bread has heated through. Serve warm.

PESTO ROLLS

Combine 1/4 cup toasted pine nuts, 2–3 tablespoons freshly grated parmesan cheese, 1–2 cloves peeled garlic, 2 tablespoons olive oil, 50 g chopped butter, 3–4 teaspoons lemon juice, 1 cup fresh basil leaves, salt and pepper, to taste, in food processor bowl. Process 20–30 seconds or until smooth. (Add a little more butter or oil if pesto is dry.) Cut 6 small dinner rolls in half vertically. Spread each half with mixture. Toast rolls under preheated grill 5–10 minutes or until heated through. Serve with shavings of parmesan cheese. Alternatively, place roll halves together; wrap in foil. Place on hot barbecue grill or flatplate, turning occasionally to ensure even cooking.

From top left: Bacon and Cheese Bread, Garlic Bread, Tomato and Olive Bread, Pesto Rolls.

CHICKEN AND CHEESE

HAM AND PINEAPPLE

SWEET CHILLI VEGETABLE

MEXICAN

Dressed-up Potatoes

To cook potatoes: Wash and scrub the required amount of large old potatoes; pat dry with paper towels. Prick potatoes all over with a fork or skewer. Wrap potatoes individually in foil. Place potatoes around hot coals of barbecue or on top grill of a preheated weber barbecue. Cook potatoes 30–60 minutes (depending on potato size). Insert a sharp knife or skewer in the centre to test if potato is cooked. (Flesh should be soft all the way through.) Remove foil from potatoes. Cut a large cross in the top of each. Squeeze to open; soften potato flesh by mashing gently with a fork. Mix a flavoured butter (such as garlic butter – see recipe below) into potato flesh and top with topping of choice. Serve hot.

Garlic Butter: (makes enough for 2 potatoes) Combine 50 g softened butter with 1–2 cloves crushed garlic. Mix well. Alternatively, add your favourite freshly chopped herbs or ground spices to butter to create your own flavoured butter.

CHICKEN AND CHEESE

Mix a small amount of garlic butter into potato flesh. Top each potato with grated cheddar cheese, shredded barbecued chicken, coleslaw, salt and pepper. Spoon over a dollop of sour cream. Sprinkle with sweet paprika. Serve hot.

Serves 1–2

MEXICAN

Heat 1 tablespoon olive oil and 20 g butter in medium pan. Add 1 finely chopped onion, 2 teaspoons dried mixed herbs, 1 clove crushed garlic, 1 teaspoon each ground cumin and coriander. Cook 2 minutes or until onion is soft. Add 200 g lean beef mince, 2 tablespoons tomato paste; cook 2–3 minutes. Stir in 1 chopped tomato, 1/4 cup canned red kidney beans, 1/4 cup bottled tomato pasta sauce; season with salt, pepper and chilli powder, to taste. Simmer 5–10 minutes to reduce liquid. Spoon over hot potato. Top with grated cheddar cheese, mashed avocado, sour cream and cheese corn chips.

Serves 1–2

HAM AND PINEAPPLE

Heat 1 teaspoon olive oil in pan. Add 1 ham steak cut in small cubes. Cook 2 minutes. Stir in 2–3 drained chopped pineapple rings and 2 finely sliced spring onions. Cook over medium heat 2 minutes or until heated through. Mix a small amount of garlic butter into potato flesh. Top with ham mixture. Sprinkle with pepper. Serve hot. Serves 1–2

HERBED SOUR CREAM

CHICKEN CURRY

BOLOGNAISE

MUSHROOM AND BACON

HERBED SOUR CREAM

Combine 1 cup sour cream, 1 tablespoon each of chopped chives, oregano and parsley, 2 teaspoons chopped mint, salt and pepper, to taste. Add 1 clove crushed garlic, if desired. Mix well. Spoon over hot potato.   Serves 2–4

SWEET CHILLI VEGETABLE

Heat 1 tablespoon sesame oil in wok. Add 1 clove crushed garlic, 1 tablespoon soy sauce, 2–3 teaspoons sweet Thai chilli sauce, 3 teaspoons plum sauce, 1 small thinly sliced carrot, 1/2 red capsicum thinly sliced, 50 g small broccoli florets, 1 small thinly sliced zucchini. Cook over medium heat 2–3 minutes. Add 2 sliced spring onions; cook 1 minute further. Season with pepper and salt. Mix a small amount of garlic butter into potato flesh. Top with the vegetables. Serve hot.   Serves 1–2

BOLOGNAISE

Heat 1 tablespoon oil in medium pan. Add 1 finely chopped onion, 1 teaspoon dried Italian mixed herbs and 1 clove crushed garlic; cook 1 minute. Add 250 g lean beef mince. Cook 3–4 minutes until browned. Add 1/2 cup bottled pasta sauce, 2 tablespoons tomato paste and 2–3 teaspoons balsamic vinegar. Cook, simmering, 3–4 minutes or until liquid has reduced. Stir in 1 tablespoon chopped fresh basil. Mix a small amount of garlic butter into potato flesh. Top with bolognaise and sprinkle with grated cheese. Serve immediately.   Serves 1–2

CHICKEN CURRY

Heat 1 tablespoon oil and 20 g butter in medium pan. Add 1 chopped onion, 1 clove crushed garlic, 2–3 teaspoons curry powder; cook 1 minute. Add 1 cup shredded barbecued chicken, 1 tablespoon sultanas and 1 small peeled, chopped green apple. Cook, stirring 2 minutes. Stir in 2 teaspoons flour. Gradually add 1/4 cup chicken stock and 2–3 tablespoons coconut cream. Stir until mixture boils and thickens. Season with salt and pepper. Spoon over potato, sprinkle with coriander leaves. Serve hot.   Serves 1–2

MUSHROOM AND BACON

Heat 30 g butter in frying pan. Add 1 clove crushed garlic, 2 finely sliced bacon rashers. Cook 1 minute. Stir in 10 large sliced mushrooms. Cook 3–4 minutes until soft. Stir in 1/4 cup cream and 1 tablespoon chopped chives. Season with salt and pepper. Cook 1 minute. Mix garlic butter into potato flesh, if desired. Spoon mixture over potato. Serve sprinkled with shavings of parmesan cheese.   Serves 1–2

Sauces

HORSERADISH CREAM

Using electric beaters, beat 125 g cream cheese until soft and creamy. Add 1 tablespoon each of mayonnaise and sour cream, 1–2 teaspoons minced horseradish or horseradish cream and 1 tablespoon chopped chives, lemon thyme or parsley. Beat until combined. Serve with fish or beef.

CHILLI BARBECUE SAUCE

Heat 20 g butter in small pan. Add 1 teaspoon ground cumin, 1/2 teaspoon each of ground coriander and paprika. Cook 30 seconds. Stir in 1 tablespoon sweet chilli sauce, 1/3 cup bottled barbecue sauce and 2 teaspoons Worcestershire sauce. Mix well. Serve with lamb or beef.

TARTARE SAUCE

Combine 1/2 cup whole egg mayonnaise, 1 tablespoon sour cream, 1–2 tablespoons halved capers and 3 teaspoons finely chopped gherkins. Add 1 tablespoon chopped fresh dill, if desired. Serve with seafood or fish.

CREAMY MUSTARD SAUCE

Combine 2 tablespoons whole egg mayonnaise, 1/3 cup sour cream, 2–3 tablespoons Dijon or wholegrain mustard. Season with salt and pepper, to taste. Mix well. (Add 1 tablespoon of your favourite fresh chopped herbs, if desired.) If sauce is too thick, add a little cream to achieve required consistency. Serve with beef or chicken.

TARTARE SAUCE

HORSERADISH CREAM

CHILLI BARBECUE SAUCE

CREAMY MUSTARD SAUCE

CORIANDER MAYONNAISE

TOMATO SAUCE

HERB GARLIC HOLLANDAISE

TOMATO SAUCE

Heat 1 tablespoon olive oil and 20 g butter in small pan. Add 1 small finely chopped onion, 1 clove crushed garlic and 1–2 teaspoons Italian dried mixed herbs. Cook 2–3 minutes or until onion is soft. Stir in 2 large chopped ripe tomatoes, 1/2 cup tomato purée and 2 teaspoons balsamic vinegar. Cook 3–4 minutes. Remove from heat. Process until smooth. Season with salt and pepper. Serve warm or cold with burgers, sausages, steak or fish.

GARLIC HERB HOLLANDAISE

Place 2 egg yolks in food processor bowl or blender. With motor constantly running, add 160 g melted butter in thin stream. Process until thick and creamy. Add 2–3 tablespoons lemon juice or white wine vinegar, 1 tablespoon each of chopped chives, basil, oregano and 1 clove crushed garlic. Season with salt and pepper. Process 10 seconds to combine. Serve with fish, seafood, chicken or beef.

CORIANDER MAYONNAISE

Place 3 egg yolks in food processor bowl or blender. With motor constantly running, add 3/4 cup light olive oil in thin stream. Process until thick and creamy. Add 2 tablespoons lemon juice and 1–2 tablespoons chopped coriander. Process until combined. Season with salt and pepper. Add crushed garlic clove if desired, or vary the taste with your own herb selection. Serve with chicken, fish or veal.

Marinades

LEMON AND WINE MARINADE

Combine 2 tablespoons lemon juice, 2 teaspoons grated lemon rind, 1 clove crushed garlic, 1/4 cup white wine, 1/4 cup olive oil, 2 tablespoons soft brown sugar, 1 tablespoon each of chopped rosemary and lemon thyme. Mix well. Marinate lamb or chicken several hours or overnight in refrigerator. Turn meat occasionally; keep covered.

LEMON AND WINE

TERIYAKI MARINADE

Combine 1/4 cup soy sauce, 2 tablespoons teriyaki sauce, 3 teaspoons grated fresh ginger, 1–2 cloves crushed garlic, 2 tablespoons soft brown sugar, 1/4 cup chicken or beef stock and 2–3 tablespoons sweet sherry. Mix well. Marinate beef, pork or chicken several hours or overnight in refrigerator. Turn meat occasionally; keep covered.

TERIYAKI

SPICED YOGHURT MARINADE

Combine 1 cup plain yoghurt, 1 finely chopped onion, 3/4 teaspoon each of ground coriander, cumin, garam masala and cinnamon, 1 clove crushed garlic, 1/2 teaspoon ground ginger, 1 teaspoon sugar, salt, pepper and pinch of cardamom. Mix well. Marinate lamb or beef several hours or overnight in refrigerator. Turn meat occasionally; keep covered.

SPICED YOGHURT

APRICOT AND ONION MARINADE

Combine 1/3 cup apricot nectar, 1 teaspoon Worcestershire sauce, 1 tablespoon each of oil and malt vinegar, 1–2 tablespoons French onion soup mix and 2–3 finely sliced spring onions. Mix well. Marinate pork or chicken several hours or overnight in refrigerator. Turn meat occasionally; keep covered. (Add 1/4 cup red or white wine to this marinade, if desired.)

APRICOT AND ONION

MUSTARD AND HERB MARINADE

Combine 1/4 cup olive oil, 2 tablespoons balsamic vinegar, 2 teaspoons soft brown sugar, 2–3 teaspoons Dijon, German or wholegrain mustard, 1–2 teaspoons mixed dried herbs, 1 tablespoon chopped fresh parsley, salt and pepper. Mix well. Marinate beef or lamb several hours or overnight in refrigerator. Turn meat occasionally; keep covered.

MUSTARD AND HERB

Dressings

HONEY GARLIC DRESSING

Combine $1/4$ cup peanut oil, 2 tablespoons lemon or lime juice, 1 teaspoon grated lemon rind, 6 teaspoons honey, 1–2 cloves crushed garlic, 1 tablespoon fresh chopped chives, salt and pepper, to taste, in screwtop jar. Shake until well combined. Pour over tossed green salad.

ORANGE AND SESAME DRESSING

Combine 1 tablespoon sesame oil, 2 tablespoons orange juice, 2 teaspoons toasted sesame seeds, 1 teaspoon grated orange rind, 1–2 teaspoons soy sauce, $3/4$ teaspoon grated ginger, salt and pepper, to taste, in screwtop jar. Shake until well combined. Pour over rocket and watercress salad.

CREAMY DRESSING

Place 2 tablespoons olive oil, 1 tablespoon mayonnaise, 1 tablespoon sour cream, 2 tablespoons lemon juice, 1 teaspoon soft brown sugar, salt and cracked black pepper, to taste, in a screwtop jar. Shake until well combined. Pour over Caesar salad. (Add 1 clove crushed garlic and 1 tablespoon chopped fresh chives to dressing, if desired.)

BASIL DRESSING

Combine $1/3$ cup basil leaves, $3/4$ teaspoon sugar, 1 clove garlic, $1/4$ cup olive or vegetable oil, 1 tablespoon white wine vinegar, 1 tablespoon grated parmesan cheese, $1/4$ cup toasted pine nuts, pepper and salt, to taste, in food processor bowl. Process until smooth. Add a little extra oil to thin, if necessary. Pour over tomato salad.

VINAIGRETTE DRESSING

Combine $1/4$ cup each of white wine vinegar and oil in a screwtop jar; season with salt and pepper, to taste. Shake until well combined. Pour over fresh garden salad. (Add 1–2 tablespoons of your favourite freshly chopped herbs to this dressing, if desired.)

HONEY GARLIC DRESSING

CREAMY DRESSING

BASIL DRESSING

ORANGE AND SESAME

VINAIGRETTE DRESSING

BURGERS & SAUSAGES

BEST-EVER BURGER WITH HOMEMADE BARBECUE SAUCE

Preparation time: 20 minutes
+ 30 minutes refrigeration
Total cooking time: 25 minutes
Serves 6

750 g beef mince
250 g sausage mince
1 small onion, finely chopped
1 tablespoon Worcestershire
    sauce
2 tablespoons tomato sauce
1 cup fresh breadcrumbs
1 egg, lightly beaten
2 large onions, extra,
    thinly sliced in rings
6 wholemeal rolls
6 small lettuce leaves
1 large tomato, sliced

Homemade Barbecue Sauce
2 teaspoons oil
1 small onion, finely chopped
3 teaspoons brown vinegar
1 tablespoon soft brown
    sugar
1/3 cup tomato sauce
2 teaspoons Worcestershire
    sauce
2 teaspoons soy sauce

➤ PLACE BEEF MINCE and sausage mince in a large bowl.

1 Add onion, sauces, breadcrumbs and egg. Using hands, mix until thoroughly combined. Divide mixture into 6 equal portions and shape into 1.5 cm thick patties. Refrigerate patties at least 30 minutes. Prepare and heat barbecue.

2 Place patties on hot lightly oiled barbecue grill or flatplate. Barbecue over hottest part of fire 8 minutes each side, turning once. While patties are cooking, fry onions on oiled flatplate until golden.

To assemble burgers: Split rolls in half. Place bases on individual serving plates. Top each base with lettuce leaf, patty, tomato slice and fried onions. Top with a generous quantity of Homemade Barbecue Sauce. Cover with remaining bun half.

3 To make Homemade Barbecue Sauce: Heat oil in a small pan. Cook onion 5 minutes or until soft. Add vinegar, sugar and sauces; stir to combine and bring to the boil. Reduce heat and simmer 3 minutes. Cool.

COOK'S FILE

Storage time: Burgers can be prepared up to 4 hours in advance and stored, covered, in refrigerator. Sauce can be made up to 1 week in advance. Store in refrigerator.

CHICKEN BURGER WITH TANGY GARLIC MAYONNAISE

Preparation time: 20 minutes
+ 3 hours marinating
Total cooking time: 15 minutes
Serves 4

4 chicken breast fillets
1/2 cup lime juice
1 tablespoon sweet chilli sauce
4 bacon rashers
4 hamburger buns
4 lettuce leaves
1 large tomato, sliced

Garlic Mayonnaise
2 egg yolks
2 cloves garlic, crushed
1 tablespoon Dijon mustard
1 tablespoon lemon juice
1/2 cup olive oil

➤ PLACE CHICKEN in a shallow, non-metal dish; prick chicken breasts with a skewer several times.

1 Combine lime juice and chilli sauce in a jug. Pour over chicken; cover. Marinate several hours or overnight. Prepare and light barbecue 1 hour before cooking. Remove and discard rind from bacon, cut bacon in half crossways.

2 Place chicken and bacon on hot lightly greased barbecue grill or flatplate. Cook bacon 5 minutes or until crisp. Cook chicken another 5–10 minutes until well browned and cooked through, turning once. Cut hamburger buns in half and toast each side until lightly browned. Top bases with lettuce, tomato, chicken and bacon. Top with Garlic Mayonnaise; finish with remaining bun top.

3 To make Garlic Mayonnaise: Place egg yolks, garlic, mustard and lemon juice in food processor bowl or blender. Process until smooth. With motor constantly running, add the oil in a thin, steady stream. Process until mayonnaise reaches a thick consistency. Refrigerate, covered, until required.

COOK'S FILE

Storage time: Chicken can be marinated up to 1 day ahead. Store mayonnaise up to 1 month in refrigerator.
Variation: For a tangy mayonnaise substitute lemon juice for lime juice and omit garlic.

1

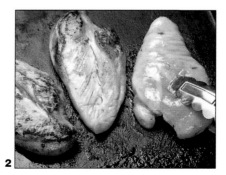

2

3

MUSTARD BURGER WITH TOMATO AND ONION SALAD

Preparation time: 20 minutes
Total cooking time: 10 minutes
Makes 8 patties

1 kg beef mince
1/4 cup seeded mustard
2 teaspoons Dijon mustard
1 teaspoon beef stock powder
1 cup stale breadcrumbs
1 egg
1 teaspoon black pepper
1/4 cup chopped red capsicum

Tomato and Onion Salad
1 small red onion
4 tomatoes
2 tablespoons red wine vinegar
1 1/2 teaspoons caster sugar
2 teaspoons lemon juice

➤ PREPARE AND HEAT barbecue. Place beef mince in large bowl.
1 Add mustards, stock powder, breadcrumbs, egg, pepper and capsicum; mix well with hands. Divide mixture into 8 portions.
2 Shape portions into round patties. Cook on hot lightly greased barbecue grill or flatplate 2–3 minutes each side, turning once. Serve with Tomato

and Onion Salad and bread of choice.
3 To make Tomato and Onion Salad: Chop onion and tomatoes into small cubes. Combine in bowl with vinegar, sugar and juice; mix well.

C O O K ' S   F I L E

Storage time: Patties can be prepared 1 day ahead. Store, covered, in refrigerator and barbecue just before serving. Salad can be made 1 day ahead. Store, covered, in refrigerator
Hint: Substitute any mustard for Dijon mustard. German or American mustard will make a mild-tasting burger. English mustard makes a strong-tasting, hot burger.

19

APRICOT GLAZED SAUSAGES AND ONIONS

Preparation time: 20 minutes
Total cooking time: 15–20 minutes
Serves 4–6

3 onions
8 thick beef sausages
1 teaspoon seeded mustard
1 cup dried apricot halves
3/4 cup apricot nectar

➤ PREPARE AND HEAT barbecue.
1 Cut onions in half; slice thinly. Cook onions on lightly greased barbecue flatplate 5 minutes or until soft. Transfer to a plate; keep warm. Place sausages on barbecue flatplate and cook 5 minutes or until well browned, turning frequently.
2 Slice sausages lengthways, three-quarters of the way through. Cook, cut-side down, a further 5 minutes or until browned. Add mustard, apricots and onions to sausages; stir.

3 Add nectar to sausage, apricot and onion mixture, a little at a time. Stir until nectar coats the sausages and begins to thicken. Repeat this process until all nectar is used. Serve sausages cut-side up, topped with onion and apricot mixture.

COOK'S FILE

Storage time: This recipe is best made just before serving.
Note: A barbecue flatplate is essential to this recipe.

HERB BURGER

Preparation time: 20 minutes
Total cooking time: 15–20 minutes
Makes 8 burgers

750 g minced beef or lamb
2 tablespoons chopped fresh
   basil
1 tablespoon chopped fresh
   chives
1 tablespoon chopped fresh
   rosemary
1 tablespoon chopped fresh
   thyme
2 tablespoons lemon juice
1 cup stale breadcrumbs
1 egg
pinch salt
pinch pepper
2 long crusty bread sticks
lettuce leaves
2 tomatoes, sliced
bottled tomato sauce

➤ PREPARE AND HEAT barbecue.
Place mince in bowl.
1 Combine mince with herbs, juice,
breadcrumbs, egg, salt and pepper.
Mix with hands until well combined.
Divide mixture into 8 portions.
2 Shape portions into thick rectangu-
lar patties about 15 cm long. Place on
hot barbecue flatplate or grill. Cook
5–10 minutes each side until well
browned and just cooked through.
3 Cut each bread stick into 4 sections.
Cut each piece in half, horizontally.
Top bases with lettuce, tomato,
herb burger and tomato sauce.
Finish with bread tops. Serve
immediately.

COOK'S FILE

Storage time: Mince mixture can be
made 1 day ahead. Refrigerate.

LENTIL AND CHICKPEA BURGER WITH CORIANDER GARLIC CREAM

Preparation time: 30 minutes
Total cooking time: 20 minutes
Makes 10 burgers

1 cup red lentils
1 tablespoon oil
2 onions, sliced
1 tablespoon tandoori mix powder
425 g can chickpeas, drained
1 tablespoon grated fresh ginger
1 egg
1/4 cup chopped fresh parsley
2 tablespoons chopped fresh coriander
2 1/4 cups stale breadcrumbs
flour, for dusting

Coriander Garlic Cream
1/2 cup sour cream
1/2 cup cream
1 clove garlic, crushed
2 tablespoons chopped fresh coriander
2 tablespoons chopped fresh parsley

➤ PREPARE AND HEAT barbecue. Bring large pan of water to the boil.
1 Add lentils to boiling water and simmer uncovered 8 minutes or until tender. Drain well. Heat oil in pan, cook onions until tender. Add tandoori mix; stir until fragrant; cool the mixture slightly.
2 Place chickpeas, half the lentils, ginger, egg and onion mixture in food processor bowl. Process 20 seconds or until smooth. Transfer to a bowl. Stir in remaining lentils, parsley, coriander and breadcrumbs; combine well. Divide mixture into 10 portions.

3 Shape portions into round patties. (If mixture is too soft, refrigerate 15 minutes or until firm.) Toss patties in flour. Shake off excess. Place patties on hot lightly greased barbecue grill or flatplate. Cook 3–4 minutes each side or until browned, turning once. Serve with Coriander Garlic Cream.
To make Coriander Garlic Cream: Combine sour cream, cream, garlic and herbs in bowl; mix well.

COOK'S FILE

Storage time: Patties can be prepared up to 2 days ahead and stored, covered, in refrigerator. Cream can be made up to 3 days ahead. Store, covered, in refrigerator.
Note: This recipe can be served as a vegetarian dish on its own, or as an interesting accompaniment to other meat dishes. Coriander Cream is delicious with chicken or fish burgers.

1

2

3

HONEY SOY SAUSAGES

Preparation time: 15 minutes
  + overnight marinating
Total cooking time: 5–6 minutes
Serves 4–6

8–10 thick beef or pork
  sausages
3 cm piece fresh ginger
1/3 cup honey
1/3 cup soy sauce
1 clove garlic, crushed
1 tablespoon sweet sherry
2 sprigs fresh thyme

➤ PLACE SAUSAGES in a large bowl or shallow non-metal dish.
1 Peel ginger and grate finely. Combine honey, soy sauce, ginger, garlic, sherry and thyme in jug; mix well.
2 Pour marinade over sausages. Cover and refrigerate overnight to allow flavours to be absorbed.
3 Prepare and heat barbecue 1 hour before cooking. Lightly grease barbecue grill or flatplate. Cook sausages 5–6 minutes, away from the hottest part of the fire, brushing occasionally with marinade. Turn sausages frequently to prevent marinade burning. (Marinade should form a thick, slightly sticky glaze around the sausages.) Serve with barbecued pineapple slices, if desired.

COOK'S FILE

Storage time: Sausages can be marinated up to 2 days in advance. Store in refrigerator.
Hints: Buy sausages made from pure beef or pork. They are tastier and less fatty than the cheaper variety.
Honey Soy Marinade can also be used over chicken, beef or lamb. Marinate overnight for best results.

LAMB BURGER WITH MANGO, CORIANDER AND MINT SALSA

Preparation time: 30 minutes
Total cooking time: 10–15 minutes
Makes 8 patties

425 g can mangoes
1 kg lamb mince
1 small red onion, finely chopped
1 tablespoon chopped fresh
   coriander
1 egg
1 cup stale breadcrumbs
2 tablespoons sweet chilli sauce
1/4 teaspoon salt

Mango Salsa
1/2 small red onion, chopped
1 tablespoon chopped fresh mint
1 tablespoon chopped fresh
   coriander leaves
2/3 cup finely chopped cucumber
1 tablespoon white wine vinegar
1 small red chilli, chopped
2 teaspoons sugar
salt and pepper to taste

➤ PREPARE AND HEAT barbecue. Lightly grease barbecue plate. Drain mangoes, reserving 1 tablespoon syrup. Cut mangoes into 1 cm cubes.
1 Combine mince, onion, coriander, egg, breadcrumbs, chilli sauce and salt in bowl. Add 1/4 cup of the mango;

mix until well combined. Divide into 8 portions. Shape into patties.
2 Place patties on hot lightly oiled barbecue flatplate. Cook 5 minutes each side or until cooked through. Serve with Mango Salsa.
3 To make Mango Salsa: Combine remaining mango and syrup with onion, herbs, cucumber, vinegar, chilli, sugar, salt and pepper in bowl; mix well.

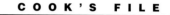
COOK'S FILE

Storage time: Patties can be prepared a day ahead and stored, covered, in refrigerator.
Hint: Salsa can also be served as a dip; mix through a little plain yoghurt and serve with chunks of fresh bread.

HERB AND GARLIC SAUSAGE WITH RED ONION RELISH

Preparation time: 20 minutes
Total cooking time: 40 minutes
Serves 4

4 herb and garlic sausages
25 cm square focaccia
4 lettuce leaves, shredded
1 medium tomato, sliced

Red Onion Relish
2 tablespoons olive oil

2 medium red onions, sliced
2 teaspoons malt vinegar
1 tablespoon sugar

➤ PREPARE AND HEAT barbecue.
1 Place sausages on hot, lightly oiled barbecue grill or flatplate. Barbecue, turning frequently, 10 minutes or until well browned and cooked through. Cut sausages in half, lengthways.
2 Cut focaccia into quarters, split in half horizontally and toast under preheated grill each side until golden. Place lettuce and tomato on each focaccia base, followed by sausage. Top with Red Onion Relish. Cover

with remaining focaccia squares. Serve with grilled peppers, if desired.
3 To make Red Onion Relish: Heat oil in medium pan, cook onions over medium-low heat 15 minutes, stirring frequently, until very soft but not browned. Add vinegar and sugar; cook a further 10 minutes. Serve warm or at room temperature.

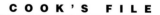
COOK'S FILE

Storage time: Relish can be made up to 1 day in advance.
Hint: Use any of the wide variety of flavoured sausages now available from butchers or some supermarkets.

Lamb Burger with Mango, Coriander and Mint Salsa (top)
Herb and Garlic Sausage with Red Onion Relish.

BREAKFAST SKEWERS WITH QUICK TOMATO SAUCE

Preparation time: 25 minutes
Total cooking time: 35 minutes
Serves 4

4 beef sausages
16 small button mushrooms
4 rashers bacon
4 lamb kidneys
30 g butter, melted
4 large tomatoes, halved

Quick Tomato Sauce
1 tablespoon oil
1 small onion, finely chopped
3 medium tomatoes, peeled,
  finely chopped
1/4 cup barbecue sauce

➤ PREPARE AND HEAT barbecue.
1 Place sausages in a large pan, cover with cold water and bring slowly to simmering point. Leave to cool. Drain well and cut each sausage into six pieces.
2 Wipe mushrooms clean with paper towels. Chop bacon into bite-size pieces. Trim kidneys, remove core and cut into quarters.
3 Thread sausage, bacon, kidney and mushrooms alternately on skewers. Place skewers on hot lightly oiled barbecue flatplate, brush with melted butter and cook 15 minutes, turning occasionally, or until browned and cooked through. Place tomatoes on hot grill cut-side down; cook 5 minutes. Serve skewers with tomatoes and Quick Tomato Sauce.
4 To make Quick Tomato Sauce: Heat oil in a small pan. Cook onion over medium-low heat 5 minutes until soft; add tomatoes and sauce. Cook 10 minutes, stirring occasionally. Serve warm or at room temperature.

COOK'S FILE

Storage time: Sauce can be made up to 1 day in advance.
Hints: If using wooden skewers, soak in cold water 1 hour before assembling. This will help to prevent the wood burning during cooking.
Serve this dish with scrambled eggs and wholemeal English muffins for a hearty breakfast.

1

2

3

4

BARBECUED HOT DOGS WITH CREAMY SLAW

Preparation time: 20 minutes
Total cooking time: 10 minutes
Serves 6

6 large thick, spicy
    frankfurts
1 tablespoon oil
6 hot dog rolls
6 small lettuce leaves

Creamy Slaw
100 g red cabbage
100 g green cabbage
2 spring onions
1/2 cup whole egg mayonnaise
1 tablespoon German mustard

➤ PREPARE AND HEAT barbecue.
1 Make 4 diagonal cuts in each frankfurt, slicing halfway through. Brush frankfurts with oil, and cook on hot lightly oiled barbecue flatplate 7–10 minutes or until cooked through.
2 Split rolls lengthways through the centre top; line with lettuce leaf. Place Creamy Slaw on lettuce, and top with hot dog. Serve immediately.
3 To make Creamy Slaw: Finely shred cabbage; finely chop spring onions. Combine mayonnaise with mustard. Place all ingredients in medium mixing bowl and toss to combine thoroughly.

COOK'S FILE

Storage time: Slaw can be made up to 4 hours in advance. Barbecue frankfurts just before serving.

CHILLI BURGER WITH AVOCADO SALSA

Preparation time: 25 minutes
Total cooking time: 10 minutes
Serves 6

1 kg beef mince
1 small onion, finely chopped
3 teaspoons chopped chilli
1 teaspoon ground cumin
2 tablespoons tomato paste
2 tablespoons chopped coriander
6 bread rolls
6 lettuce leaves

Avocado Salsa
1 medium avocado
2 tablespoons lime juice
1 small tomato, chopped
130 g can corn kernels, drained

➤ PREPARE AND HEAT barbecue. Place mince in a large mixing bowl.

1 Add onion, chilli, cumin, tomato paste and coriander. Using hands, mix until thoroughly combined. Divide mixture into 6 equal portions and shape into 1.5 cm thick patties.

2 Place patties on hot lightly oiled grill or flatplate. Barbecue 4–5 minutes each side, turning only once. Serve between split bread rolls with lettuce and Avocado Salsa.

3 To make Avocado Salsa: Peel avocado and remove stone. Cut into small cubes, place in a bowl and toss immediately with lime juice. Add tomato and corn and lightly combine.

COOK'S FILE

Storage time: Patties can be prepared up to 4 hours in advance.
Hint: The quantity of chilli in this recipe will produce quite spicy burgers. If you prefer a milder taste, reduce chilli to 2 teaspoons.

PORK SAUSAGE BURGER WITH MUSTARD CREAM

Preparation time: 20 minutes
Total cooking time: 15 minutes
Serves 6

1 kg pork mince
1 small onion, finely
    chopped
1 cup fresh breadcrumbs
2 cloves garlic, crushed
1 egg, lightly beaten

1 teaspoon dried sage
6 long crusty bread rolls

Mustard Cream
1/2 cup sour cream
1 tablespoon wholegrain mustard
2 teaspoons lemon juice

➤ PREPARE AND HEAT barbecue. Place mince in large mixing bowl.
1 Add onion, breadcrumbs, garlic, egg and sage. Using hands, mix to combine thoroughly. Divide the mixture into 6 equal portions, shape into sausage shapes about 16 cm long.
2 Place burgers on hot, lightly oiled barbecue flatplate or grill. Barbecue 5–10 minutes, turning occasionally. Place on a long crusty roll with Mustard Cream. Garnish with chives and serve with a salad, if desired.
3 To make Mustard Cream: Place sour cream, mustard and juice in a small bowl and stir to combine.

COOK'S   FILE

Storage time: Burgers can be prepared up to 4 hours in advance.

CHEESE-STUFFED BURGER WITH RED SALSA

Preparation time: 25 minutes
+ 1 hour standing
Total cooking time: 20 minutes
Serves 6

1 kg beef mince
1 small onion, finely chopped
2 tablespoons chopped parsley
1 teaspoon dried oregano
1 tablespoon tomato paste
70 g cheddar cheese
6 white bread rolls
lettuce leaves

Red Salsa
2 medium red capsicum
1 medium ripe tomato, finely
    chopped
1 small red onion, finely
    chopped
1 tablespoon olive oil
2 teaspoons red wine vinegar

➤ PREPARE AND HEAT barbecue.
1 Place mince in large mixing bowl; add onion, herbs and tomato paste. Using hands, mix until thoroughly combined. Divide mixture into 6 equal portions and shape into patties. Cut cheese into small squares. Make a cavity in the top of each patty with thumb. Place cheese in cavity and smooth mince over to enclose the cheese completely.
2 Place patties on hot lightly oiled barbecue grill or flatplate. Barbecue 4–5 minutes each side, turning once. Remove from barbecue; keep warm. Split each roll in half; place a lettuce leaf on the base of each, top with pattie and Red Salsa.
3 To make Red Salsa: Trim capsicum, remove seeds and membrane.

Cut into wide pieces and place skin-side up under a hot grill. Cook 4–5 minutes or until skin blisters and blackens. Cover with damp tea-towel and leave to cool. Remove skin from capsicum and finely chop flesh. Combine with tomato, onion, olive oil and vinegar and stand at least 1 hour to allow flavours to develop. Serve salsa at room temperature.

COOK'S FILE

Storage time: Burgers can be prepared up to 4 hours in advance. Salsa can be made up to 1 day in advance. Store, covered, in refrigerator.
Variation: Camembert, brie or blue cheese can be used to stuff patties, if desired. Substitute bottled tomato sauce or ready-made salsa, available from supermarkets, if time is short.

1

2

3

BURGER WITH THE WORKS

Preparation time: 40 minutes
Total cooking time: 10–15 minutes
Serves 6

750g lean beef mince
1 onion, finely chopped
1 egg
1/2 cup fresh breadcrumbs
2 tablespoons tomato paste

1 tablespoon Worcestershire
  sauce
2 tablespoons chopped fresh
  parsley
salt and cracked pepper, to taste
3 large onions
30 g butter
6 slices cheddar cheese
6 eggs, extra
6 rashers bacon
6 large hamburger buns, lightly
  toasted

shredded lettuce
2 tomatoes, thinly sliced
6 large slices beetroot, drained
6 pineapple rings, drained
tomato sauce

➤ PREPARE AND HEAT barbecue.
1 Combine mince, onion, egg, breadcrumbs, tomato paste, Worcestershire sauce, parsley, salt and pepper in large bowl. Mix with hands until well combined.
2 Divide mixture into 6 portions. Shape each portion into round patties 1.5 cm thick. Cover and set aside. Slice onions into thin rings. Heat butter on hot barbecue flatplate. Cook onions, turning often until well browned. Move onions towards outer edge of flatplate to keep warm. Brush barbecue grill or flatplate liberally with oil.
3 Cook meat patties 3–4 minutes each side or until browned and cooked through. Move patties to cooler part of barbecue or transfer to plate and keep warm. Place slice of cheese on each patty. (The heat of the burger will be enough to partially melt the cheese.) Heat a small amount of butter in a large frying pan. Fry eggs and bacon until eggs are cooked through and bacon is golden and crisp. Remove from heat.
To assemble burgers: Place toasted bun bases on individual serving plates. Top each with lettuce, tomato, beetroot and pineapple. Place cooked meat patty on top, followed by cooked onions, egg, bacon and tomato sauce. Place remaining bun halves on top. Serve with potato chips, if desired.

COOK'S FILE

Storage time: Burgers can be prepared up to 4 hours in advance. Refrigerate until needed. Burger best prepared just before serving.

1

2

3

BEEF, LAMB & PORK

TANGY BEEF RIBS

Preparation time: 20 minutes
 + 3 hours marinating
Total cooking time: 15–20 minutes
Serves 4

1 kg beef ribs
1/2 cup tomato sauce
2 tablespoons Worcestershire
  sauce
2 tablespoons soft brown sugar
1 teaspoon paprika
1/4 teaspoon chilli powder
1 clove garlic, crushed

➤ CHOP RIBS into individual serving pieces, if necessary. Bring a large pan of water to boil.

1 Cook ribs in boiling water 5 minutes; drain.

2 Combine tomato sauce, Worcestershire sauce, sugar, paprika, chilli powder and garlic in large bowl and mix well. Add ribs to sauce. Cover and marinate, in refrigerator, several hours or overnight. Prepare and heat barbecue 1 hour before cooking.

3 Cook ribs on hot lightly greased barbecue grill or flatplate 10–15 minutes, brushing frequently with marinade, or until ribs are well browned and cooked through. Serve with favourite barbecued vegetables or slices of grilled fresh pineapple, if desired.

COOK'S FILE

Storage time: Ribs are best cooked just before serving.

Hint: If time is short combine ribs with marinade and leave at room temperature, covered, for up to 2 hours. The meat will absorb the flavours of the marinade more quickly at room temperature. (This principle applies to all marinades.)

Note: Ribs can be bought as a long piece or cut into individual pieces. If chopping ribs yourself you will need a sharp cleaver. Alternatively, ribs can be cooked in one piece and chopped into pieces after cooking, when the bone is softer. A longer cooking time will be required if cooked as a single piece.

Pork ribs can also be used in this recipe. Use either the thick, meaty ribs, which are like beef ribs, or the long thin spare ribs, also known as American-style ribs. Pork spare ribs have less meat so less cooking is required. They can be eaten with the fingers, so are ideal picnic food.

Veal ribs are extremely tender and are sometimes available from specialty butchers.

STEAK IN RED WINE

Preparation time: 10 minutes
  + 3 hours marinating
Total cooking time: 5–10 minutes
Serves 4

750 g rump steak
1 cup good red wine
2 teaspoons garlic salt
1 tablespoon dried oregano leaves
cracked black pepper, to taste

➤ CUT STEAKS into large, even-sized serving pieces.

1 Trim meat of excess fat and sinew.

2 Combine wine, salt, oregano leaves and pepper in a jug. Place steak in a large, shallow non-metal dish. Cover and refrigerate several hours or overnight. Prepare and heat barbecue 1 hour before cooking.

3 Cook steak on hot lightly greased barbecue grill or flatplate 3–4 minutes each side or until cooked as desired, brushing with wine mixture frequent-ly. Serve with potato salad and corn on the cob, if desired.

COOK'S FILE

Storage time: Steak is best cooked just before serving.

Hint: Choose a basting brush with pure bristles. Nylon bristles can melt in the heat and introduce an unpleas-ant flavour to cooked foods.

Variation: Substitute 2 tablespoons of fresh oregano for dried oregano, if desired.

1

2

3

HOT PEPPERED STEAKS WITH HORSERADISH SAUCE

Preparation time: 15 minutes
Total cooking time: 10 minutes
Serves 4

4 (800 g) medium-sized sirloin
    steaks
1/4 cup seasoned, cracked
    pepper

Horseradish Sauce
2 tablespoons brandy
1/4 cup beef stock
1/3 cup cream
1 tablespoon horseradish cream
1/2 teaspoon sugar
salt and pepper, to taste

➤ PREPARE AND HEAT barbecue. Lightly grease barbecue grill. Trim meat of excess fat and sinew.

1 Coat steaks on both sides with pepper, pressing it firmly into the meat.

2 Barbecue steaks 5–10 minutes until cooked as desired. Serve with Horseradish Sauce and steamed vegetables, such as crisp snow peas.

3 To make Horseradish Sauce: Combine brandy and stock in pan. Bring to boil, reduce heat. Stir in cream, horseradish and sugar and stir until heated through. Season to taste.

COOK'S FILE

Storage time: Steaks best cooked close to serving.

FILLET STEAK WITH FLAVOURED BUTTERS

Preparation time: 30 minutes
Total cooking time: 15 minutes
Serves 4

4 fillet steaks (500 g)

Garlic Butter
125 g butter
3 cloves garlic, crushed
2 spring onions, finely
   chopped

Capsicum & Herb Butter
1 small red capsicum
125 g butter
2 teaspoons chopped oregano
2 teaspoons chopped chives
salt and pepper, to taste

➤ PREPARE AND HEAT barbecue. Lightly grease barbecue plate. Trim steaks of excess fat and sinew. Using a sharp knife, cut a pocket in side of each steak.

1 To make Garlic Butter: Beat butter in bowl until creamy, add garlic and chopped spring onions; beat until smooth.

To make Capsicum & Herb Butter: Cut capsicum in half. Remove seeds and membrane. Place cut-side down on cold grill tray. Brush skin with oil. Cook under pre-heated hot grill until skin blisters and blackens. Remove from grill. Cover with damp tea-towel. Cool. Peel away skin and discard. Finely chop capsicum flesh. Beat butter until creamy. Add capsicum, herbs, salt and pepper; beat until smooth.

2 Push 2–3 teaspoons Garlic Butter into two of the steaks; push 2–3 teapoons Capsicum & Herb Butter into remaining steaks.

3 Cook on hot barbecue grill or flat-plate 4–5 minutes each side, turning once. Brush steaks frequently with any remaining flavoured butter while cooking.

COOK'S FILE

Storage time: Prepare steak 1 day ahead and store in refrigerator. Butters will keep 2 weeks in refrigerator, provided they are well covered.

BEEF SATAY STICKS WITH PEANUT SAUCE

Preparation time: 30 minutes
+ 3 hours marinating
Total cooking time: 10–15 minutes
Serves 4

800 g rump steak
1/3 cup soy sauce
2 tablespoons oil
2 cloves garlic, crushed
1 teaspoon grated ginger

Peanut Sauce
1 cup pineapple juice
1 cup peanut butter
1/2 teaspoon garlic powder
1/2 teaspoon onion powder
2 tablespoons sweet chilli sauce
1/4 cup soy sauce

➤ TRIM STEAK of excess fat and sinew.

1 Slice meat across the grain evenly into long, thin strips. Thread meat strips onto skewers, bunching them thickly along three-quarters of the skewer; place satays in a shallow, non-metal dish.

2 Combine soy sauce, oil, garlic and ginger in a small jug: pour over satays. Store in refrigerator, covered with plastic wrap, several hours or overnight, turning occasionally. Prepare and heat barbecue 1 hour before cooking. Place skewers on hot lightly oiled grill or flatplate. Barbecue 8–10 minutes or until tender, turning occasionally. Serve with Peanut Sauce.

3 To make Peanut Sauce: Combine juice, peanut butter, garlic and onion powders and sauces in a small pan and stir over medium heat 5 minutes or until smooth. Serve warm.

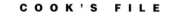

COOK'S FILE

Storage time: Barbecue satay sticks just before serving. Sauce can be made 1 day in advance. If sauce has thickened, add a little warm water when reheating.

Variation: The quantity of chilli sauce may be altered to taste, or use chopped fresh chilli for extra spice.

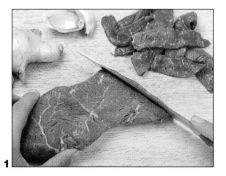

1

2

3

LAMB CUTLETS WITH ROSEMARY MARINADE

Preparation time: 15 minutes
  + 20 minutes marinating
Total cooking time: 6–8 minutes
Serves 4

12 lamb cutlets
2 tablespoons fresh chopped
    rosemary
1/4 cup olive oil
1 1/2 teaspoons cracked black
    pepper
1 bunch fresh rosemary, extra

➤ PREPARE AND HEAT barbecue.
1 Trim cutlets of excess fat and sinew. Place cutlets in shallow, non-metal dish and brush with oil.
2 Scatter half the chopped rosemary and pepper on meat; set aside for 20 minutes. Turn meat over and brush with remaining oil, scatter over remaining rosemary and pepper. Tie the extra bunch of rosemary to the handle of a wooden spoon.
3 Arrange cutlets on hot lightly greased grill. Cook 2–3 minutes each side. As cutlets cook, bat frequently with the rosemary spoon. This will release flavoursome oils into the cutlets. When cutlets are almost done, remove rosemary from the spoon and drop it on the fire where it will flare up briefly and infuse rosemary smoke into the cutlets. Serve with barbecued lemon slices, if desired.

COOK'S FILE

Storage time: Cook cutlets just before serving.
Variation: This dish is ideal for a barbecue picnic. Marinate and pack in a sealed container with rosemary sprigs. Add sprigs to the fire, as described above.

1

2

3

LAMB CHOPS WITH PINEAPPLE SALSA

Preparation time: 20 minutes
Total cooking time: 10 minutes
Serves 6

12 lamb loin chops
2 tablespoons oil
1 teaspoon cracked black
   pepper

Pineapple Salsa
1/2 ripe pineapple (or 400 g
   drained canned pineapple)
1 large red onion

1 fresh red chilli
1 tablespoon cider or rice
   vinegar
1 teaspoon sugar
salt and black pepper, to taste
2 tablespoons chopped mint

➤ PREPARE AND HEAT barbecue.
1 Trim meat of excess fat and sinew. Brush chops with oil and season with pepper.
2 To make Pineapple Salsa: Peel pineapple; remove core and eyes. Cut into 1 cm cubes. Peel onion, finely chop. Slit open chilli, scrape out seeds. Chop chilli flesh finely. Combine pineapple, onion and chilli in medium

bowl; mix lightly. Add vinegar, sugar, salt, pepper and mint; mix well.
3 Place lamb chops on lightly greased barbecue grill or flatplate. Cook chops 2–3 minutes each side, turning once, until just tender. Serve with Pineapple Salsa, baked potatoes and green salad, if desired.

COOK'S FILE

Storage: Chops are best barbecued just before serving. Salsa can be made 1 day in advance and refrigerated. Add herbs just before serving. (Red onion may affect colour of pineapple.)
Hint: Pineapple Salsa will also complement grilled tuna or salmon.

LAMB SATAYS WITH CHILLI PEANUT SAUCE

Preparation time: 25 minutes
  + 1 hour marinating
Total cooking time: 15 minutes
Serves 4

600 g lamb fillets
2 cloves garlic, crushed
1/2 teaspoon ground black
    pepper
6 teaspoons finely chopped
    lemon grass
2 tablespoons soy sauce
2 teaspoons sugar
1/4 teaspoon ground turmeric

Chilli Peanut Sauce
1 1/2 cups unsalted roasted
    peanuts
2 tablespoons vegetable oil
1 medium onion, roughly
    chopped
1 clove garlic, roughly chopped
1 tablespoon sambal oelek
1 tablespoon soft brown sugar
1 tablespoon kecap manis
    (sweet soy sauce) or soy
    sauce
1 teaspoon grated ginger
1 1/2 teaspoons ground coriander
1 cup coconut cream
1/4 teaspoon ground turmeric
salt and pepper, to taste

➤ TRIM LAMB of excess fat and
sinew.
1 Cut lamb into thin strips, thread
onto skewers, bunching strips along
three-quarters of the length. Place
satays in shallow non-metal dish.
Combine garlic, pepper, lemon grass,
soy sauce, sugar and turmeric in a
small bowl; mix well. Brush marinade
over skewered meat, set aside for
1 hour. Prepare and heat barbecue.

2 To make Chilli Peanut Sauce:
Process peanuts in food processor
bowl 10 seconds or until coarsely
ground. Heat oil in small pan. Add
onion and garlic, cook over medium
heat 3–4 minutes or until translucent.
Add sambal oelek, sugar, kecap
manis, ginger and coriander. Cook
stirring 2 minutes. Add coconut
cream, turmeric and processed
peanuts. Reduce heat, cook 3 minutes
or until thickened; season with salt
and pepper. Remove from heat.
3 Place mixture in food processor
bowl. Process 20 seconds or until
almost smooth. Spoon into individual
serving dishes to cool. Barbecue

satays on hot lightly greased grill or
flatplate 2–3 minutes each side or
until browned.

COOK'S FILE

Storage time: Barbecue satays just
before serving. Satays can be marinated up to 2 days in advance. Store,
covered, in refrigerator. Sauce can be
made 3–4 days in advance. Store in a
screwtop jar in refrigerator.
Variation: Salted roasted peanuts
can be used in Chilli Peanut Sauce.
(Taste sauce before adding any addi-
tional salt.)
Hint: Chilli Peanut Sauce can be used
over any beef or vegetable satays.

1

2

3

LAMB KOFTA KEBABS WITH TAHINI DRESSING

Preparation time: 25 minutes
Total cooking time: 10 minutes
Serves 4–6

600 g lean lamb
1 medium onion, roughly chopped
2 cloves garlic, roughly chopped
1 teaspoon cracked black pepper
1½ teaspoons ground cumin
½ teaspoon ground cinnamon
1 teaspoon sweet paprika
1 teaspoon salt
2 slices bread, crusts removed, quartered

1 egg, lightly beaten
olive oil, for coating

Tahini Dressing
2 tablespoons tahini (sesame paste)
3 teaspoons lemon juice
1 small garlic clove, crushed
pinch of salt
2–3 tablespoons water
2 tablespoons sour cream
1 tablespoon chopped fresh parsley

➤ TRIM MEAT of any excess fat and sinew. Cut into small pieces suitable for processing. Prepare and heat barbecue.
1 Place lamb, onion, garlic, pepper, cumin, cinnamon, paprika, salt, bread and egg in food processor bowl.

Process 20–30 seconds or until mixture becomes a smooth paste.
2 Divide mixture into 12. Using oil-coated hands, shape portions into sausages. Wrap sausages around skewers; refrigerate until needed.
To make Tahini Dressing: Combine tahini, lemon juice, garlic, salt, water, sour cream and parsley in small bowl. Stir until creamy.
3 Arrange kofta kebabs on hot lightly greased barbecue grill or flat-plate. Cook 10 minutes, turning frequently, until browned and cooked through. Serve with Tahini Dressing and grilled tomato halves, if desired.

COOK'S FILE

Storage time: Cook kebabs just before serving. Tahini Dressing can be made a day ahead.

PORK LOIN CHOPS WITH APPLE CHUTNEY

Preparation time: 20 minutes
+ 3 hours marinating
Total cooking time: 25 minutes
Serves 6

6 pork loin chops
2/3 cup white wine
2 tablespoons oil
2 tablespoons honey
1 1/2 teaspoons ground
    cumin
2 cloves garlic, crushed

Apple Chutney
3 medium green apples

1/2 cup apple juice
1/2 cup fruit chutney
15 g butter

➤ TRIM PORK CHOPS of excess fat and sinew.

1 Combine wine, oil, honey, cumin and garlic in small jug; mix well. Place chops in shallow non-metal dish; pour marinade over. Store, covered with plastic wrap, in refrigerator several hours or overnight, turning occasionally. Prepare and heat barbecue 1 hour before cooking.

2 Place chops on hot lightly oiled barbecue grill or flatplate. Cook 8 minutes each side or until tender, turning once. Serve immediately with Apple Chutney.

3 To make Apple Chutney: Peel apples and cut into small cubes. Place in small pan; cover with apple juice. Bring to the boil, reduce heat and simmer, covered, 7 minutes or until completely soft. Add chutney and butter; stir to combine. Serve warm.

COOK'S FILE

Storage time: Chops can be marinated up to 1 day in advance. Barbecue just before serving. Apple Chutney can be made 1 day in advance. Store, covered, in refrigerator and reheat gently to serve.

Hint: Apple Chutney can be used on roast pork, lamb chops, chicken cutlets or as a relish with a cheese plate. Serve warm or cold.

1

2

3

GINGER-ORANGE PORK STEAKS

Preparation time: 15 minutes
+ 3 hours marinating
Total cooking time: 20 minutes
Serves 6

6 pork butterfly steaks (200 g
    each)
1 cup ginger wine
1/2 cup orange marmalade
2 tablespoons oil
1 tablespoon grated ginger

➤TRIM PORK STEAKS of excess fat and sinew.

1 Combine wine, marmalade, oil and ginger in small jug; mix well. Place steaks in shallow non-metal dish; pour marinade over. Store, covered with plastic wrap, in refrigerator several hours or overnight, turning occasionally. Prepare and heat barbecue 1 hour before cooking. Drain pork steaks; reserve marinade.

2 Place pork on hot lightly oiled barbecue grill or flatplate. Cook 5 minutes each side or until tender, turning once.

3 While meat is cooking, place

reserved marinade in small pan. Bring to the boil; reduce heat and simmer 5 minutes until marinade has reduced and thickened slightly. Pour over pork steaks immediately.

COOK'S FILE

Storage time: This recipe best barbecued close to serving.

Hint: Steaks of uneven thickness may curl during cooking. To prevent this, leave a layer of fat on the outside of the steak and make a few, deep cuts in the fat prior to cooking. Remove fat before serving.

1

2

3

Pork Loin Chops with Apple Chutney (top)
Ginger-Orange Pork Steaks.

SWEET AND SOUR MARINATED PORK KEBABS

Preparation time: 30 minutes
  + 3 hours marinating
Total cooking time: 20 minutes
Serves 6

1 kg pork fillets
1 large red capsicum
1 large green capsicum
425 g can pineapple pieces
1 cup orange juice
¼ cup white vinegar
2 tablespoons soft brown sugar
2 teaspoons chilli garlic sauce
2 teaspoons cornflour

➤ TRIM PORK of excess fat and sinew.

1 Cut meat into 2.5 cm cubes. Cut both capsicum into 2 cm squares. Drain pineapple and reserve juice. Thread meat, alternately with capsicum and pineapple, onto skewers. Combine reserved pineapple juice with orange juice, vinegar, sugar and sauce. Place kebabs in a shallow non-metal dish, pour half the juice mixture over. Refrigerate, covered with plastic wrap, several hours or overnight, turning occasionally. Prepare and heat barbecue 1 hour before cooking.

2 To make Sweet and Sour Sauce: Place remaining marinade in small pan. Mix cornflour with a table-spoon of the marinade in small bowl until smooth; add to pan. Stir over medium heat until mixture boils and thickens; transfer to small serving bowl. Cover surface with plastic wrap; leave to cool.

3 Place meat on a hot lightly oiled barbecue grill or flatplate and cook 15 minutes, turning occasionally, until tender. Serve kebabs with Sweet and Sour Sauce.

COOK'S FILE

Storage time: Kebabs can be marinated up to 1 day in advance.
Note: Chilli garlic sauce is available from Asian food shops and some supermarkets.

1

2

3

BARBECUED PORK SPARE RIBS

Preparation time: 15 minutes
+ 3 hours marinating
Total cooking time: 30 minutes
Serves 4–6

1 kg American-style pork spare
  ribs
2 cups tomato sauce
1/2 cup sherry
2 tablespoons soy sauce
2 tablespoons honey
3 cloves garlic, crushed
1 tablespoon grated fresh
  ginger

➤ TRIM SPARE RIBS of excess fat and sinew.

1 Cut racks of ribs into pieces, so that each piece has three or four ribs. Combine tomato sauce, sherry, soy sauce, honey, garlic and ginger in a large pan; mix well.

2 Add ribs to mixture. Bring to the boil. Reduce heat and simmer, covered, 15 minutes. Move ribs occasionally to ensure even cooking. Transfer ribs and sauce to shallow non-metal dish; allow to cool. Refrigerate, covered with plastic wrap, several hours or overnight. Prepare and heat barbecue 1 hour before cooking.

3 Place ribs on hot lightly oiled barbecue grill or flatplate. Cook over

the hottest part of the fire 15 minutes, turning and brushing with sauce occasionally. Serve with barbecued corn on the cob and potato salad, if desired.

COOK'S FILE

Storage time: Ribs can be prepared up 2 days in advance. Store, covered, in the refrigerator. Barbecue just before serving.

Note: American-style pork spare ribs come in rack form. They can be eaten easily with the fingers if they are separated into individual ribs. Serve ribs with other pre-dinner finger foods next to a dipping sauce, such as barbecue or tomato, and a generous supply of napkins.

CHICKEN

HONEY GLAZED CHICKEN BREASTS

Preparation time: 6 minutes
  + 20 minutes marinating
Total cooking time: 10 minutes
Serves 6

6 chicken breast
    fillets (1 kg)
50 g butter, softened
1/4 cup honey
1/4 cup barbecue sauce
2 teaspoons seeded mustard

➤ TRIM CHICKEN of excess fat and sinew. Remove skin.

1 Use a sharp knife to make three or four diagonal slashes across one side of each chicken breast. Prepare and heat barbecue.

2 Combine butter, honey, barbecue sauce and mustard in a small bowl. Spread half of the marinade thickly over the slashed side of the chicken; cover. Set remaining marinade aside. Stand chicken at room temperature 20 minutes.

3 Place chicken breasts, slashed-side up, on hot, lightly greased grill or flat-plate. Cook 2–3 minutes each side or until tender. Brush with reserved marinade several times during cooking. Serve hot with buttered ribbon noodles, if desired.

COOK'S FILE

Storage time: Barbecue chicken just before serving. Chicken can be marinated overnight, provided that it is kept, covered, in the refrigerator. The longer the chicken is marinated, the more it will take on flavour, so if chicken is not desired overly sweet, marinate for a short time only.

Hints: Crisply fried onion is an appealing accompaniment to this dish. Peel 4 medium onions, cut in half and slice finely. Heat 4 cups of good quality vegetable oil or olive oil to medium-hot. Place onion in a frying basket, lower into the oil. (If oil begins to foam, lift basket out, set aside 30 seconds, then try again.) Cook 10–15 minutes or until onion is well browned and crisp. Drain on paper towels. Serve immediately.

Leftover cooked chicken can be shredded and served mixed through a green salad or sliced thickly and made up into sandwiches for a picnic.

Notes: When honey is cooked, its sugars caramelise and some of its flavour is lost. For a distinctive taste to this dish, use honeys with a strong, dark flavour, such as leather-wood, lavender or rosemary. Lighter honeys, such as yellow box, orange blossom or clover, will sweeten and glaze the meat without necessarily affecting its flavour. Usually the paler the honey, the milder its flavour.

If honey crystallises, place the jar in a pan of warm water and turn gently until liquefied. Honey should be stored in a cool, dry place. (It will become grainy if refrigerated.)

THAI CHICKEN CUTLETS

Preparation time: 20 minutes
    + 1 hour marinating
Total cooking time: 20 minutes
Serves 4–6

12 chicken thigh
    fillets (1.25 kg)
6 cloves garlic
1 teaspoon black
    peppercorns
3 coriander roots and stems,
    roughly chopped
1/4 teaspoon salt

Chilli Garlic Dip
4–5 dried red chillies
2 large cloves garlic, chopped
1/4 cup sugar
1/3 cup cider or rice vinegar
pinch salt
1/4 cup boiling water

➤ PREPARE AND HEAT barbecue.
1 Trim chicken of excess fat and sinew.
2 Place garlic, peppercorns, coriander and salt in food processor bowl. Process 20–30 seconds or until the mixture forms a smooth paste. (This can also be done using a mortar and pestle.) Place chicken in shallow non-metal dish. Spread garlic mixture over chicken. Stand chicken at room temperature 1 hour.
3 To make Chilli Garlic Dip: Soak chillies in hot water 20 minutes. Drain chillies and chop finely. Place in a mortar with garlic and sugar. Grind to a smooth paste. Place mixture in a small pan. Add vinegar, salt and water. Bring to boil, reduce heat, simmer 2–3 minutes. Cool.
4 Barbecue chicken on hot greased grill or flatplate 5–10 minutes each side, turning once. Serve with Chilli Garlic Dip.

COOK'S FILE

Storage: Chicken can be marinated, in refrigerator, 1 day in advance. Dip can be made 3 days in advance.
Hint: Serve chicken with a salad of sliced cucumber and shredded carrot and radish marinated in white vinegar, sugar and salt. The sweet-tart flavour of the salad complements the spiciness of the chicken.

1

2

3

4

MIDDLE EASTERN BAKED CHICKEN

Preparation time: 30 minutes
Total cooking time: 1 hour 15 minutes
Serves 6

1.6 kg chicken
1/2 cup boiling water
1/2 cup instant couscous
4 pitted dates, chopped
4 dried apricots, chopped
1 tablespoon lime juice
1 tablespoon olive oil
20 g butter
1 medium onion, chopped
1–2 cloves garlic, chopped
1 teaspoon salt
1/4 teaspoon cracked black
    pepper
1 teaspoon ground coriander
2 tablespoons chopped
    parsley
salt and pepper, extra
1 teaspoon ground cumin
1 tablespoon olive oil,
    extra

➤ PREPARE AND HEAT weber (kettle) barbecue for indirect cooking. (See page 7.) Place drip tray underneath top grill.

1 Remove giblets and any large deposits of fat from chicken. Wipe and pat dry chicken with paper towel. Pour boiling water over couscous and set aside 15 minutes for couscous to swell and soften. Soak dates and apricots in lime juice; set aside.

2 Heat oil and butter in pan, add onion and garlic; cook 3–4 minutes until translucent. Remove from heat; add couscous and soaked dried fruit, salt, pepper, coriander and parsley. Mix well. Spoon stuffing into chicken cavity and close with toothpicks or a skewer. Tie legs together with string.

3 Rub chicken skin all over with combined salt, pepper, cumin and extra oil. Place chicken in the centre of a large piece of greased foil. Gather edges of foil and wrap securely.

4 Place the parcel on barbecue grill over drip tray. Cover barbecue, cook 50 minutes. Open the foil, crimping the edges to form a tray to retain most of the cooking liquids. Cook a further 20 minutes or until chicken is tender and golden. Remove from heat and stand 5–6 minutes before carving.

COOK'S FILE

Storage: Bake chicken just before serving. Chicken can be stuffed 3–4 hours in advance.

Hint: Leftover chicken can be sliced and served with a salad of avocado, sliced onion and orange segments.

CHICKEN CUTLETS WITH CORN RELISH

Preparation time: 20 minutes
Total cooking time: 25 minutes
Serves 4

8 chicken thigh cutlets,
    skin on (1 kg)
1 tablespoon olive oil
1 small clove garlic, crushed
1/4 teaspoon ground turmeric
1/2 teaspoon salt

Corn Relish
1 cup frozen or canned corn
    kernels
1 tablespoon olive oil
1 red chilli, seeded and chopped
1 small green capsicum, finely
    chopped
1 medium onion, finely chopped
1/3 cup white vinegar
1/4 cup sugar
1 teaspoon seeded mustard
1/2 cup water
3 teaspoons cornflour
1 teaspoon paprika
1 teaspoon finely chopped fresh
    coriander leaves
1 tablespoon olive oil, extra

➤ PREPARE AND HEAT barbecue. Trim chicken of excess fat and sinew.
1 Prick skin of cutlets with point of a knife. Place cutlets in large frying pan of boiling water. Reduce heat, simmer 5 minutes. Remove from pan; drain. Cool. Combine olive oil, garlic, turmeric and salt and rub over the skin side of the cutlets. Set aside.
2 To make Corn Relish: Cook corn in pan of boiling water 2–3 minutes or until tender; drain. (If using canned corn, drain, but do not cook.) Heat oil in medium pan. Add chilli, capsicum and onion. Cook over medium heat until tender. Add corn, vinegar, sugar and mustard, and cook stirring further 5 minutes. Add blended water and cornflour. Bring to boil, reduce heat, stir until thickened. Stir in paprika, coriander and remaining extra oil. Remove from heat; cool.
3 Place cutlets, skin-side up, on hot lightly greased barbecue grill or flatplate. Cook 2 minutes; turn and cook skin side 4 minutes. Continue cooking another 5–10 minutes, turning frequently until the chicken is well browned and cooked through. Serve with Corn Relish.

COOK'S FILE

Storage time: Relish can be made up to 4 days in advance, stored in a jar and refrigerated.

CHICKEN KEBABS WITH CURRY MAYONNAISE

Preparation time: 25 minutes
+ 30 minutes marinating
Total cooking time: 10 minutes
Serves 4

600 g chicken breast fillets
4 large spring onions
1 small green capsicum
1 small red capsicum
1/4 cup olive oil
1 teaspoon freshly ground black
   pepper
1/2 teaspoon ground turmeric
1 1/2 teaspoons ground
   coriander

Curry Mayonnaise
3/4 cup whole egg mayonnaise
1 tablespoon hot curry powder
1/4 cup sour cream

1 tablespoon sweet fruit or
   mango chutney, mashed
1/4 cup finely chopped, peeled
   cucumber
1/2 teaspoon toasted cumin seeds
1 tablespoon finely chopped
   fresh mint
1 teaspoon finely chopped fresh
   mint, extra

➤ PREPARE AND HEAT barbecue. Trim chicken of excess fat and sinew.

1 Cut chicken into 3 cm cubes. Trim spring onions, cut white stems and thicker parts of green stems into 3 cm lengths; discard tops. Cut red and green capsicum into 3 cm squares.

2 Thread chicken, spring onions and red and green capsicum onto skewers, using at least two pieces of each. Arrange kebabs, side by side, in shallow, non-metal dish. Combine oil, pepper, turmeric and coriander in a jug. Pour over kebabs; set

aside 30 minutes at room temperature.

3 To make Curry Mayonnaise: Combine mayonnaise, curry powder, sour cream, chutney, cucumber, cumin seeds and mint in a bowl; mix well. Spoon into a dish or jug for serving. Sprinkle mayonnaise with extra chopped mint.

Place kebabs on hot lightly oiled barbecue grill or flatplate. Cook 2–3 minutes each side or until cooked through and tender. Serve Curry Mayonnaise separately.

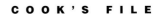

COOK'S FILE

Storage time: Kebabs can be assembled 4 hours ahead. Barbecue just before serving. Mayonnaise can be made 1 day ahead and stored in refrigerator. Sprinkle with extra mint just before serving.

Hint: Serve kebabs with rice and fried pappadums, or wrapped in sheets of Lebanese bread.

CITRUS CHICKEN DRUMSTICKS

Preparation time: 20 minutes
+ 3 hours marinating
Total cooking time: 20 minutes
Serves 4

8 chicken drumsticks
1/3 cup orange juice
1/3 cup lemon juice
1 teaspoon grated orange rind
1 teaspoon grated lemon rind
1 teaspoon sesame oil
1 tablespoon olive oil
1 spring onion, finely chopped

➤ WASH DRUMSTICKS and pat dry with paper towels.

1 Trim any excess fat and score thickest part of chicken with a knife. Place in a shallow non-metal dish.

2 Combine juices, rinds, oils and spring onion in jug, pour over chicken. Store, covered with plastic wrap, in refrigerator several hours or overnight, turning occasionally. Drain chicken, reserve marinade. Prepare and heat barbecue 1 hour before cooking.

3 Cook drumsticks on hot lightly oiled barbecue grill or flatplate 15–20 minutes or until tender. Brush occasionally with the reserved marinade. Serve immediately.

COOK'S FILE

Storage time: This dish is best cooked just before serving.

TANDOORI WEBER CHICKEN

Preparation time: 15 minutes
+ 4 hours marinating
Total cooking time: 1 hour
Serves 4

4 chicken marylands (drumstick and thigh), skin removed
1 teaspoon salt
2 cloves garlic, crushed
1 tablespoon lemon juice
1 cup plain yoghurt
1 1/2 teaspoons garam masala
1/2 teaspoon ground black pepper
1/2 teaspoon ground turmeric
2–3 drops red food colouring
olive oil, for basting
20–30 mesquite or hickory chips, for smoking

➤ PLACE MARYLANDS in a non-metal dish; rub with salt and garlic.

1 Combine lemon juice, yoghurt, garam masala, pepper and turmeric in a jug. Add food colouring to make the marinade a bright orange-red colour. Pour over the chicken, and coat evenly with the back of a spoon. Cover, set aside 4 hours, turning chicken every hour and redistributing the marinade. During the last hour of marinating, heat and prepare weber (kettle) barbecue for indirect cooking (see page 7).

2 When barbecue coals are covered with fine white ash, add mesquite or hickory chips to coals. Cover the barbecue and leave until the smoke is well established (about 5 minutes).

3 Brush barbecue grill with oil. Arrange marylands on grill; put lid on barbecue. Smoke-cook 45 minutes–1 hour or until chicken is well crisped. Brush chicken with oil several times during cooking. Serve with side salad and onion rings, if desired.

COOK'S FILE

Storage time: Cook the chicken just before serving.
Note: Tandoori chicken requires a slow heat. Do not place chicken on barbecue while the fire is still very hot. Test the heat of the fire before adding the chips. Hold your hand over the top grill. If you can leave your hand, comfortably, for 4–5 seconds the fire is low enough to use. If fire is too hot, allow to burn down 15–30 minutes more.

Citrus Chicken Drumsticks (top)
Tandoori Weber Chicken.

BUFFALO CHICKEN WINGS WITH RANCH DRESSING

Preparation time: 25 minutes
+ 3 hours marinating
Total cooking time: 10 minutes
Serves 4

8 large chicken wings (900 g)
2 teaspoons black pepper
2 teaspoons garlic salt
2 teaspoons onion powder
olive oil, for deep frying
1/2 cup tomato sauce
2 tablespoons Worcestershire
   sauce
20 g butter, melted
2 teaspoons sugar
Tabasco sauce, to taste

Ranch Dressing
1/2 cup whole egg mayonnaise
1/2 cup sour cream
2 tablespoons lemon juice
2 tablespoons chopped chives
salt and white pepper, to taste

➤ WASH WINGS thoroughly and pat dry with paper towels.

1 Cut tips off each wing; discard. Bend each wing back to snap joint and cut through to create two pieces. Combine pepper, garlic salt and onion powder. Using fingers, rub mixture into each piece.

2 Heat oil to moderately hot in deep heavy-based pan. Cook chicken pieces in batches 2 minutes; remove with tongs or slotted spoon and drain on paper towels.

3 Transfer chicken to non-metal bowl or shallow dish. Combine sauces, butter, sugar and Tabasco and pour over chicken; stir to coat. Refrigerate, covered, several hours or overnight. Prepare and heat barbecue 1 hour before cooking.

4 Place chicken on hot lightly oiled barbecue grill or flatplate. Cook 5 minutes, turning and brushing with marinade. Serve with Ranch Dressing.

To make Ranch Dressing: Combine mayonnaise, cream, juice, chives, salt and pepper in bowl, mix well.

COOK'S FILE

Storage time: Wings can be prepared up to 2 days in advance.

CHICKEN BURGER WITH TARRAGON MAYONNAISE

Preparation time: 25 minutes
Total cooking time: 20 minutes
Serves 6

1 kg chicken mince
1 small onion, finely chopped
2 teaspoons lemon rind
2 tablespoons sour cream
1 cup fresh breadcrumbs
6 onion bread rolls

Tarragon Mayonnaise
1 egg yolk
1 tablespoon tarragon vinegar
1/2 teaspoon French mustard
1 cup olive oil
salt and white pepper, to taste

➤ PREPARE AND HEAT barbecue. Place chicken mince in a mixing bowl.
1 Add onion, rind, sour cream and breadcrumbs. Using hands, mix until thoroughly combined. Divide mixture into 6 equal portions and shape into 1.5 cm thick patties.
2 Place patties on hot lightly oiled barbecue grill or flatplate. Cook 7 minutes each side, turning once. Serve on an onion roll with salad fillings and Tarragon Mayonnaise.
3 To make Tarragon Mayonnaise: Place yolk, half the vinegar and the mustard in a small mixing bowl. Whisk together 1 minute until light and creamy. Add oil about 1 teaspoon at a time, whisking constantly until mixture thickens. Increase flow of oil to a thin stream; continue whisking until all the oil has been incorporated. Stir in remaining vinegar and salt and white pepper.

COOK'S FILE

Storage time: Burgers can be prepared up to 1 day in advance and mayonnaise up to 4 hours in advance. Store both in refrigerator.
Variation: Mayonnaise can also be made in the food processor. Add the oil in a thin stream, with motor constantly running, until the mixture thickens and turns creamy.
Note: Do not use black pepper in mayonnaise as it will discolour the mixture.

1

2

3

CHICKEN BREASTS WITH FRUIT MEDLEY

Preparation time: 25 minutes
  + 3 hours marinating
Total cooking time: 20 minutes
Serves 4

4 chicken breast fillets
3/4 cup white wine
1/4 cup olive oil
2 teaspoons grated ginger
1 clove garlic, crushed

Fruit Medley
225 g can pineapple slices, drained
1 small mango, peeled
2 small kiwi fruit, peeled
150 g watermelon, peeled, seeds
  removed
1 tablespoon finely chopped
  fresh mint

➤ TRIM CHICKEN of fat and sinew.
1 Place chicken in shallow non-metal dish. Combine wine, oil, ginger and garlic in a jug; pour over chicken. Refrigerate, covered with plastic wrap, several hours or overnight, turning occasionally. Prepare and light barbecue 1 hour before cooking.
2 Place chicken fillets on hot lightly oiled barbecue grill or flatplate. Cook 5–10 minutes each side, or until well browned on the outside. Serve immediately with Fruit Medley and barbecued onion slices, if desired.
3 **To make Fruit Medley:** Chop fruit finely and combine with mint in small serving bowl.

COOK'S FILE

Storage time: Chicken can be marinated up to 2 days in advance. Medley can be made up to 2 hours in advance.
Variation: Substitute any of the fruits with your favourite fruits in season. Use at least one ingredient with a firm flesh, for example, apple or pear.

TANDOORI SKEWERS

Preparation time: 20 minutes
  + 3 hours marinating
Total cooking time: 10 minutes
Serves 4–6

1 kg chicken thigh fillets
1 cup plain yoghurt
1 teaspoon chilli powder
1 teaspoon turmeric
1 teaspoon ground cumin
1 teaspoon ground
  coriander
1 teaspoon grated ginger
1 clove garlic, crushed

➤ TRIM CHICKEN of excess fat and sinew.
1 Cut each thigh fillet into thin strips; weave onto small skewers, bunching the chicken along about three-quarters of the length.
2 Combine yoghurt, spices, ginger and garlic; mix well. Place skewers in shallow non-metal dish, cover with yoghurt mixture and refrigerate, covered with plastic wrap, several hours or overnight, turning occasionally. Prepare and heat barbecue 1 hour before cooking.
3 Place chicken on hot lightly oiled barbecue grill or flatplate. Cook 8–10 minutes or until tender.

COOK'S FILE

Storage time: Skewers can be marinated up to 2 days in advance and cooked just before serving.
Note: Thighs are dark meat and will remain slightly pink even when cooked. To ensure that the chicken cooks evenly, do not bunch the meat too tightly on the skewer. Test chicken for doneness by removing from flame and piercing to the middle with a skewer. Chicken is done when juices run clear.
Hint: Serve chicken with a sauce of plain yoghurt, chopped cucumber and a pinch of cumin, or accompany chicken with a selection of sweet chutneys.

Chicken Breasts with Fruit Medley (top)
Tandoori Skewers.

TERIYAKI CHICKEN WINGS

Preparation time: 15 minutes
  + 3 hours marinating
Total cooking time: 13 minutes
Serves 4

8 chicken wings
1/4 cup soy sauce
2 tablespoons sherry
2 teaspoons grated ginger
1 clove garlic, crushed
1 tablespoon honey

➤ WASH CHICKEN wings and pat dry with paper towel.

1 Trim any excess fat from wings, and tuck tips under to form a triangle.

2 Place wings in shallow non-metal dish. Combine soy sauce, sherry, ginger, garlic and honey in a jug; mix well. Pour over chicken. Store, covered with plastic wrap, in refrigerator several hours or overnight. Prepare and light barbecue 1 hour before cooking. Lightly brush two sheets of aluminium foil with oil. Place 4 wings in a single layer on each piece of foil; wrap completely.

3 Place parcels on hot barbecue grill or flatplate 10 minutes. Remove parcels from heat; unwrap. Place wings directly on lightly greased grill 3 minutes or until brown. Turn wings frequently and brush with any remaining marinade.

COOK'S FILE

Storage time: Chicken can be marinated up to 2 days in advance. Cook just before serving.

Variation: Marinade can also be used on beef or pork.

Note: Teriyaki marinade is available in the Asian section of most supermarkets or Asian food shops.

CHICKEN FAJITAS

Preparation time: 35 minutes
+ 3 hours marinating
Total cooking time: 10 minutes
Serves 4

4 chicken breast fillets
2 tablespoons olive oil
1/4 cup lime juice
2 cloves garlic, crushed
1 teaspoon ground cumin
1/4 cup chopped fresh coriander
    leaves
8 flour tortillas
1 tablespoon olive oil, extra
2 medium onions, sliced
2 medium green capsicum, cut
    into thin strips
1 cup grated cheddar cheese
1 large avocado, sliced
1 cup bottled tomato salsa

➤ TRIM CHICKEN of fat and sinew.
1 Cut chicken into thin strips. Place in shallow non-metal dish. Combine oil, juice, garlic, cumin and coriander in jug; mix well. Pour over chicken. Store, covered, in the refrigerator several hours or overnight. Prepare and heat barbecue 1 hour before cooking.
2 Wrap tortillas in foil and place on a cool part of the barbecue grill for 10 minutes to warm through. Heat oil on flatplate. Cook onion and capsicum for 5 minutes or until soft. Push over to a cooler part of the plate to keep warm.
3 Place chicken and marinade on flatplate and cook 5 minutes until just tender. Transfer chicken, vegetables and wrapped tortillas to serving platter. Make up individual fajitas by placing chicken, cooked onion and capsicum, grated cheese and avocado over flat tortillas. Top with salsa. Roll up to enclose filling.

COOK'S FILE

Storage time: Chicken can be marinated up to 2 days in advance.
Note: Tomato salsa is available from supermarkets and comes in hot, medium or mild forms.

SEAFOOD

SALMON CUTLETS WITH FRUIT SALSA

Preparation time: 20 minutes
+ 3 hours marinating
Total cooking time: 10 minutes
Serves 4

4 salmon cutlets
6 teaspoons seasoned pepper
2 tablespoons lemon juice
1/2 cup lime juice
1 tablespoon chopped fresh
  thyme

Fruit Salsa
1/2 small pawpaw, peeled
1/4 small pineapple, peeled
3 spring onions, chopped
1 tablespoon chopped fresh
  coriander
2 tablespoons lime juice
3 teaspoons caster sugar
salt, to taste

► SPRINKLE SALMON cutlets all over with seasoned pepper.
1 Place salmon cutlets in shallow non-metal dish. Combine lemon juice, lime juice and thyme in small jug. Pour over salmon cutlets. Cover and refrigerate several hours.
2 Place salmon on hot lightly greased barbecue grill or flatplate; brush with any remaining marinade. Cook 5–10 minutes each side, turning once, until outside is lightly browned and flesh is just cooked on the inside. Serve with Fruit Salsa.

3 To make Fruit Salsa: Chop pawpaw and pineapple into 1 cm cubes. Combine in medium bowl with spring onions, coriander, lime juice, caster sugar and salt.

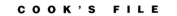

COOK'S FILE

Storage time: Barbecue salmon just before serving. Do not marinate for more than 3 hours as the citrus juices will begin to 'cook' the fish and turn the flesh opaque. If this should occur reduce the cooking time by half. Salsa should be made just before serving.
Notes: Salmon cutlets are expensive, so choose only the very best. Look for cutlets with bright-orange flesh, that are firm to the touch, with a clear, dry bone. The skin should be pale grey.
When purchashing pawpaw (papaya) look for a deep yellow skin colour and a firm flesh. (If pawpaw yields easily to gentle pressure in the thickest area, it is over-ripe and should not be used.)
Smaller pawpaws with orange-red flesh (sometimes known as Mountain Papayas) are generally available at the beginning of summer. Their flesh is more delicate than the large variety.
Store uncut, ripe pawpaws in the refrigerator up to 7 days. Serve as soon as possible after cutting. Leftover pawpaw flesh can be peeled and chopped, covered with lemon juice, and stored in the refrigerator for up to 3 days. Alternatively, purée remaining flesh and freeze in ice-cube trays to use in fruit drinks.

CAJUN CALAMARI

Preparation time: 15 minutes
+ 3 hours marinating
Total cooking time: 5 minutes
Serves 4

600 g large calamari (or squid)
   hoods
1/4 cup lemon juice
2 cloves garlic, crushed
2 teaspoons tomato paste
1 teaspoon garam masala
2 teaspoons ground coriander
2 teaspoons paprika
2 teaspoons seasoned pepper
2 teaspoons caster sugar
1 tablespoon grated
   fresh ginger
1 tablespoon olive oil
1/4 teaspoon ground nutmeg
pinch chilli powder

➤ WASH CALAMARI thoroughly, removing any membrane. Pat dry with paper towel.

1 Using a sharp knife, cut through one side of each hood, open out to give a large, flat piece of flesh. With inside facing up, score flesh diagonally, in a criss-cross pattern, taking care not to cut all the way through. Against the grain of those cuts, slice flesh into long strips about 2 cm thick.

2 Combine juice, garlic, tomato paste, spices, sugar, ginger, oil, nutmeg and chilli in bowl; mix well. Add calamari strips; stir to combine. Cover and refrigerate several hours or overnight. Prepare and heat barbecue 1 hour before cooking.

3 Cook calamari and marinade on hot lightly greased barbecue flatplate 5 minutes or until flesh curls and turns white. Remove from the heat and serve immediately.

COOK'S FILE

Storage time: Calamari can be marinated up to 2 days in advance.

LEMON AND HERB TROUT

Preparation time: 20 minutes
Total cooking time: 15 minutes
Serves 4

1/4 cup chopped fresh dill
2 tablespoons chopped fresh
    rosemary
1/3 cup coarsely chopped fresh
    continental (flat-leaf) parsley
2 teaspoons thyme leaves
6 teaspoons crushed green
    peppercorns
1/3 cup lemon juice
salt and pepper, to taste
2 lemons
4 whole fresh trout
1/3 cup dry white wine

Horseradish Cream
1 tablespoon horseradish cream
1/2 cup sour cream
2 tablespoons cream
salt and pepper, to taste

Lemon Sauce
2 egg yolks
150 g butter, melted
3–4 tablespoons lemon juice
salt and pepper, to taste

➤ PREPARE AND HEAT barbecue.
Lightly grease four large sheets of foil,
each double-thickness.
1 Combine herbs, peppercorns, juice,
salt and pepper in bowl; mix well. Cut
each lemon into eight slices, cut each
slice in half. Place 2 lemon pieces in
each fish cavity. Spoon herb mixture
into fish cavity.
2 Place each fish on foil layers, sprinkle each with 1 tablespoon of wine.
Seal fish in foil to form neat parcels.
Cook fish on barbecue 10–15 minutes
or until fish is just cooked through.
(Test fish for doneness by gently flaking back flesh with a fork.) Stand fish,
still wrapped in foil, 5 minutes, then
serve with Horseradish Cream and
Lemon Sauce.
3 To make Horseradish Cream:
Combine creams, salt and pepper in
bowl; mix well.
To make Lemon Sauce: Place
yolks in food processor. Process
20 seconds or until blended. With
motor constantly running, add butter
slowly in a thin, steady stream.
Continue processing until all butter
has been added and mixture is thick
and creamy. Add juice, season with
salt and pepper.

COOK'S FILE

Storage time: Prepare fish parcels
1 day ahead and store in refrigerator.

GARLIC KING PRAWNS

Preparation time: 10 minutes
  + 3 hours marinating
Total cooking time: 5 minutes
Serves 4

500 g green king prawns

Marinade
2 tablespoons lemon juice
2 tablespoons sesame oil
2 cloves garlic, crushed
2 teaspoons grated fresh ginger

➤ REMOVE HEADS from prawns.
1 Peel and devein prawns, leaving tails intact. (Reserve the heads and shell for fish stock, if you like.) Make a cut in the prawn body, slicing three-quarters of the way through the flesh from head to tail.
To make Marinade: Combine juice, oil, garlic and ginger in jug; mix well.
2 Place prawns in bowl; pour on marinade and mix well. Cover and refrigerate several hours or overnight. Prepare and light barbecue 1 hour before cooking.
3 Cook prawns on hot, lightly greased flatplate 3–5 minutes or until pink in colour and cooked through. Brush frequently with marinade while cooking. Serve immediately.

COOK'S FILE

Storage time: Prawns are best barbecued close to serving. Prawns should always be cooked and eaten within 24 hours of purchase.
Variation: The quantity of garlic can be altered to taste. For a stronger flavour, double the quantity of garlic and omit the ginger, if preferred. For a hot and spicy dish, substitute 2 finely chopped fresh chillies for the garlic.

CHARGRILLED BABY OCTOPUS

Preparation time: 15 minutes
+ 3 hours marinating
Total cooking time: 5 minutes
Serves 4

1 kg baby octopus
¾ cup red wine
2 tablespoons balsamic
  vinegar
2 tablespoons soy sauce

2 tablespoons hoisin sauce
1 clove garlic, crushed

➤ WASH OCTOPUS thoroughly and wipe dry with paper towel.
1 Use a small sharp knife to slit open the head; remove the gut. Grasp the body firmly and push the beak out with your index finger. Remove and discard beak. If octopus are large, cut tentacles in half.
2 Place octopus in large bowl. Combine wine, vinegar, sauces and garlic in a jug; pour over octopus and

stir to coat completely. Cover, refrigerate several hours or overnight. Prepare and heat barbecue 1 hour before cooking.
3 Drain octopus; reserve marinade. Cook octopus on hot, lightly greased flatplate 3–5 minutes until octopus flesh turns white. Pour over the reserved marinade while cooking. Serve warm or cold.

COOK'S FILE

Storage time: Octopus can be marinated up to 2 days in advance.

HONEYED PRAWN AND SCALLOP SKEWERS

Preparation time: 15 minutes
  + 3 hours marinating
Total cooking time: 5 minutes
Makes 8 skewers

500 g medium green prawns
250 g fresh scallops
    with corals intact
1/4 cup honey
2 tablespoons soy sauce

1/4 cup bottled barbecue sauce
2 tablespoons sweet sherry

➤ SOAK EIGHT WOODEN skewers in water.
1 Remove heads from prawns. Peel and devein prawns, keeping tails intact. Clean scallops, removing brown vein.
2 Thread prawns and scallops alternately onto 8 skewers (about 3 of each per skewer). Place in base of shallow non-metal dish. Combine honey, sauces and sherry in jug and pour over skewers. Cover and refrigerate several hours or overnight. Prepare and heat barbecue 1 hour before cooking.
3 Cook skewers on hot lightly greased barbecue flatplate 5 minutes or until cooked through. Brush frequently with marinade while cooking.

COOK'S FILE

Storage time: Store marinated skewers in refrigerator for up to 2 days. Cook just before serving.
Variation: Substitute cubes of firm-fleshed fish for prawns or scallops.

1

2

3

FISH PATTIES

Preparation time: 25 minutes
Total cooking time: 10 minutes
Makes 8–10 patties

750 g white fish fillets, cut into
    cubes
1 cup stale white breadcrumbs
3 spring onions, chopped
1/4 cup lemon juice
2 teaspoons seasoned pepper
1 tablespoon chopped
    fresh dill
2 tablespoons chopped fresh
    parsley
3/4 cup grated cheddar cheese
1 egg
1/2 cup plain flour, for dusting

Herbed Mayonnaise
1/2 cup mayonnaise
1 tablespoon chopped fresh
    parsley
1 tablespoon chopped fresh
    chives
2 teaspoons chopped capers

➤ PREPARE AND HEAT barbecue. Place fish in food processor bowl. Process 20–30 seconds until smooth.
1 Place minced fish in large bowl. Add breadcrumbs, spring onions, juice, pepper, herbs, cheese and egg. Mix well. Divide into 8–10 portions. Shape into round patties. Place on tray and refrigerate 15 minutes or until firm.
2 Toss patties in flour, shake off excess. Cook patties on hot lightly greased barbecue flatplate 2–3 minutes each side until browned and cooked through. Serve with Herbed Mayonnaise and a green salad, if desired.
3 To make Herbed Mayonnaise: Combine mayonnaise, herbs and capers in a small bowl; mix well.

COOK'S FILE

Storage time: This recipe is best made just before cooking. Patties should not be prepared more than a few hours in advance. After 2–3 hours the raw fish will begin to seep liquid which will cause the patties to fall apart during cooking.
Variation: Any firm-fleshed fish can be used in this recipe. Try whiting, perch, hake or cod.

1

2

3

Honeyed Prawn and Scallop Skewers (top)
Fish Patties.

THAI MARINATED FISH

Preparation time: 10 minutes
  + 3 hours marinating
Total cooking time: 15 minutes
Serves 4

1 medium-sized white-fleshed
    fish, cleaned and scaled
3/4 cup fresh coriander leaves
2 cloves garlic, crushed
1 tablespoon soy sauce
1 tablespoon fish sauce
1 tablespoon sweet chilli sauce

2 teaspoons sesame oil
3 spring onions, finely chopped
2 teaspoons grated fresh ginger
1 tablespoon lime juice
1 teaspoon soft brown sugar

➤ PLACE FISH in large, shallow
non-metal dish.
1 Fill fish cavity with coriander
leaves.
2 Combine garlic, soy, fish and chilli
sauces, oil, spring onions, ginger,
juice and sugar in jug; mix well. Pour
marinade over fish. Cover and refrigerate several hours. Prepare and heat

the barbecue 1 hour before cooking.
3 Cook fish on hot, lightly greased
flatplate for about 15 minutes, taking
care not to burn skin of fish. (Move
fish away from the flame and dampen
the fire if fish begins to stick to plate.)
Brush fish frequently with marinade
until flesh flakes back easily with a
fork, and has turned opaque. Serve
with egg noodles and barbecued citrus
wedges, if desired.

COOK'S FILE

Storage time: Marinate fish for no
more than 2–3 hours.

1

2

3

DILL FISH WITH LEMON BUTTER SAUCE

Preparation time: 10 minutes
+ 3 hours marinating
Total cooking time: 10 minutes
Serves 4

4 boneless white fish fillets
(perch or whiting)
6 teaspoons lemon pepper
1–2 tablespoons chopped
fresh dill
1/3 cup lemon juice

Lemon Butter Sauce
2 tablespoons lemon juice
1/2 cup cream
40 g butter, chopped
2 tablespoons chopped fresh
chives

➤ RINSE FISH under cold water.
1 Sprinkle pepper all over fillets and place in shallow non-metal dish. Combine dill and lemon juice. Pour over fish, cover and refrigerate several hours. Prepare and heat barbecue 1 hour before cooking.
2 Cook fish on hot lightly greased barbecue flatplate for 2–3 minutes each side or until flesh flakes back easily with a fork. Serve with Lemon Butter Sauce, barbecued citrus slices and a green salad, if desired.
3 To make Lemon Butter Sauce: Simmer lemon juice in a small pan until reduced by half. Add cream; stir until mixed through. Whisk in butter a little at a time until all the butter has melted; stir in chives.

COOK'S FILE

Storage time: The fish and sauce are best cooked just before serving.

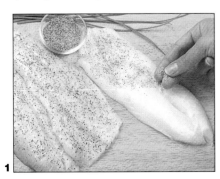
1

2

3

SWEET AND SOUR FISH KEBABS

Preparation time: 20 minutes
  + 3 hours marinating
Total cooking time: 10 minutes
Makes 12 skewers

750 g boneless white fish fillets
    (hake or cod)
225 g can pineapple pieces
1 large red capsicum
3 teaspoons soy sauce
6 teaspoons soft brown sugar
2 tablespoons white vinegar
2 tablespoons tomato sauce
salt, to taste

➤ SOAK WOODEN SKEWERS in water for several hours.

1 Cut fish into 2.5 cm cubes. Drain pineapple, reserving 2 tablespoons liquid. Cut capsicum into 2.5 cm pieces. Thread capsicum, fish and pineapple alternately onto skewers.

2 Place kebabs in shallow non-metal dish. Combine soy sauce, reserved pineapple juice, sugar, vinegar, tomato sauce and salt in small bowl; mix well. Pour marinade over kebabs. Cover; refrigerate several hours. Prepare and heat barbecue 1 hour before cooking.

3 Barbecue kebabs on hot lightly greased flatplate, brushing frequently with marinade, 2–3 minutes each side or until just cooked through. Serve immediately with cooked noodles and a dressed green salad, if desired.

COOK'S FILE

Storage time: Kebabs are best cooked just before serving. Do not marinate longer than 3 hours.
Variation: Any vegetable can be substituted for capsicum; try zucchini, cherry tomatoes, mushrooms or onion.

BARBECUED LOBSTER TAILS WITH AVOCADO SAUCE

Preparation time: 15 minutes
 + 3 hours marinating
Total cooking time: 10 minutes
Serves 4

¼ cup dry white wine
1 tablespoon honey
1 teaspoon sambal oelek
   (bottled chopped chillies)
1 clove garlic, crushed
1 tablespoon olive oil
4 (400 g) fresh green
   lobster tails

Avocado Sauce
1 medium ripe avocado, mashed
3 teaspoons lemon juice
2 tablespoons sour cream
1 small tomato, chopped finely
salt and pepper, to taste

➤ COMBINE WINE, honey, sambal oelek, garlic and oil in jug; mix well.
1 Use a sharp knife or kitchen scissors to cut along the soft shell on the underside of the lobster. Gently pull shell apart and ease raw flesh out with fingers.
2 Place lobster in shallow non-metal dish. Pour over marinade; stir well. Cover, refrigerate several hours or overnight. Prepare and light barbecue 1 hour before cooking. Cook lobster tails on hot lightly greased barbecue grill or flatplate 5–10 minutes, turning frequently. Brush with marinade until cooked through. Slice into medallions and serve with Avocado Sauce and a green salad, if desired.
3 To make Avocado Sauce: Combine avocado, juice and sour cream in bowl; mix well. Add tomato and combine with avocado mixture; add salt and pepper, to taste.

COOK'S FILE

Storage time: Avocado sauce can be made 2–3 hours ahead. Before refrigerating, press plastic wrap onto surface; this will prevent it turning black.

1

2

3

STEAMED FISH AND VEGETABLE PARCELS

Preparation time: 15 minutes
Total cooking time: 10 minutes
Serves 4

4 bream fillets
2 tablespoons horseradish
  cream
1 small tomato, finely chopped
130 g can corn kernels, drained
²/₃ cup grated cheddar cheese
1 celery stick, finely chopped
¹/₂ red capsicum, finely chopped
3 spring onions, chopped

1¹/₂ teaspoons dried mixed
  herbs
salt and pepper, to taste

➤ PREPARE AND HEAT barbecue. Grease 4 large sheets of foil, each double thickness.
1 Place a piece of fish in the centre of each piece of foil. Spread each fish fillet with a quarter of the horseradish cream.
2 Top each fillet with tomato, corn, cheese, celery, capsicum and spring onions. Sprinkle with herbs, salt and pepper. Bring foil edges together, enclosing fish in a neat parcel.
3 Cook parcels, fish-side down, on hot

barbecue grill or flatplate 5–10 minutes, without turning, until fish is cooked through. (Check fish after 5 minutes; cooked fish flakes easily and flesh has turned opaque.) Serve fish and vegetables immediately, garnished with chopped spring onions, if desired.

COOK'S FILE

Storage time: Foil parcels can be prepared several hours ahead and stored in refrigerator. Barbecue parcels just before serving.
Variation: Try other vegetables in the parcels, such as grated carrot and zucchini with finely chopped onion.

BARBECUED TUNA WITH ONIONS

Preparation time: 10 minutes
  + 3 hours marinating
Total cooking time: 10 minutes
Serves 4

4 fresh tuna steaks
4 small onions
1¹/₂ cups red wine
¹/₄ cup soft brown sugar
salt and pepper, to taste

➤ PLACE TUNA in shallow non-metal dish.

1 Cut onions in half; slice finely. Sprinkle over fish. Combine wine, sugar, salt and pepper in jug; mix well.
2 Pour marinade over fish. Cover and refrigerate several hours. Prepare and heat the barbecue 1 hour before cooking. Drain fish and onion, reserving marinade.
3 Cook tuna steaks and onions on hot lightly greased barbecue flatplate 8–10 minutes or until lightly browned and just cooked through. Pour marinade over tuna and onions a little at a time during cooking.

COOK'S FILE

Storage time: Barbecue tuna and

onions just before serving. Do not marinate for more than 3 hours.
Notes: Tuna steaks should be handled with care, as they can bruise easily at room temperature. Store in the refrigerator until ready to prepare and avoid turning or handling when marinating or cooking. Remove tuna steaks from heat as soon as they are cooked.
Hint: Tuna flesh is dark and has a strong flavour. To dilute some of this flavour without affecting the texture of the flesh, soak the steaks overnight in lightly salted water. This may whiten the flesh slightly, but will not affect its cooking time.

Steamed Fish and Vegetable Parcels (top)
Barbecued Tuna with Onions.

VEGETABLES & SALADS

MARINATED GRILLED VEGETABLES

Preparation time: 30 minutes
+ 1 hour marinating
Total cooking time: 5 minutes
Serves 6

3 small slender eggplant
2 small red capsicum
3 medium zucchini
6 medium mushrooms

Marinade
1/4 cup olive oil
1/4 cup lemon juice
1/4 cup shredded basil leaves
1 clove garlic, crushed

➤ CUT EGGPLANT into diagonal slices. Place on tray in single layer; sprinkle with salt and let stand 15 minutes. Rinse thoroughly and pat dry with paper towels.

1 Trim capsicum, removing seeds and membrane; cut into long, wide pieces. Cut zucchini into diagonal slices. Trim each mushroom stalk so that it is level with the cap. Place all vegetables in a large, shallow non-metal dish.

2 To make Marinade: Place oil, juice, basil and garlic in a small screwtop jar. Shake vigorously to combine. Pour over vegetables and combine well. Store, covered with plastic wrap, in refrigerator for 1 hour, stirring occasionally. Prepare and heat barbecue.

3 Place vegetables on hot, lightly greased barbecue grill or flatplate. Cook each vegetable piece over the hottest part of the fire 2 minutes each side. Transfer to a serving dish once browned. Brush vegetables frequently with any remaining marinade while cooking.

COOK'S FILE

Storage time: Vegetables can be marinated up to 2 hours before cooking. Take vegetables out of refrigerator 15 minutes before cooking to allow oil in marinade to soften.

Hint: Marinated Grilled Vegetables can be served warm or cold. Serve any leftover vegetables with thick slices of crusty bread or individual bread rolls.

Other herbs, such as parsley, rosemary or thyme, can be added to the marinade. This marinade can also be used as an all-purpose salad dressing. Make up extra at the time of preparation and store in the refrigerator, in a screwtop jar, for up to 2 weeks. Olive oil will solidify in the refrigerator, so allow marinade to come to room temperature before serving.

BEETROOT WITH MUSTARD CREAM DRESSING

Preparation time: 10 minutes
Total cooking time: approximately
  1 hour 15 minutes
Serves 6–8

2 rashers bacon, finely chopped
1 bunch fresh beetroot

Mustard Cream Dressing
250 g sour cream
3 teaspoons horseradish
  cream
3 teaspoons grainy mustard
1/2 teaspoon hot mustard powder
  (optional)
salt and pepper, to taste
3–4 fresh chives

➤ COOK BACON in frying pan 5–10
minutes until crisp. Drain on paper
towel and set aside.
1 Trim beetroot by removing stems
and leaves. Place in a pan; cover with
cold water. Bring to boil, reduce heat
and simmer gently 1 hour or until
beetroot are tender. (Cooking time will
depend on age and size of beetroot.)
2 Drain beetroot and set aside until
cool enough to handle. Peel; cut into
wedges. (Leave any small beetroot
whole.) Arrange in a serving bowl.
**3 To make Mustard Cream
Dressing:** Combine sour cream,
horseradish and mustard in bowl;
beat until smooth. Add hot mustard,
to taste; season with salt and pepper.
Pour dressing over the beetroot, top
with fried bacon and snipped chives.

COOK'S FILE

Storage: Beetroot can be cooked
ahead of time, peeled and stored in the
refrigerator until needed.

ROSEMARY SAUTÉED POTATOES

Preparation time: 10 minutes
Total cooking time: 25 minutes
Serves 6

4–5 large potatoes (about
    1.5 kg)
1/3 cup olive oil
1 tablespoon chopped fresh
    rosemary
1 clove garlic, crushed
salt and black pepper, to taste

➤ PEEL POTATOES and cut into 2 cm cubes.

1 Rinse the potatoes in cold water, drain well and dry thoroughly on a clean tea-towel.

2 Heat oil in large heavy-based frying pan. Add the potatoes and cook slowly, shaking pan occasionally, 20 minutes or until tender. Turn potatoes frequently to prevent sticking. Partially cover pan halfway through cooking. The steam will help to cook the potato through.

3 Add the rosemary and garlic, with salt and pepper to taste, in the last few minutes of cooking. Increase the heat to crisp the potatoes, if required.

COOK'S FILE

Storage time: Potatoes can be cooked ahead of time and reheated in a heavy-based pan moistened with olive oil, over the barbecue.

Note: Potatoes can be cooked on a large barbecue flatplate, provided the heat is not too intense. If the potatoes cook too quickly, the surface will burn without cooking through to the centre. Parboil cubed potatoes 2–5 minutes before barbecuing, if desired.

1

2

3

MARINATED ONION, CUCUMBER AND CARROT SALAD

Preparation time: 20 minutes
   + 2 hours 15 minutes marinating
Total cooking time: Nil
Serves 8

2 Lebanese cucumbers (350 g)
1 teaspoon salt
1 large onion (350 g), finely
   sliced
1/4 cup white vinegar
1/2 cup water

2 1/2 teaspoons sugar
2 teaspoons salt, extra
2 large carrots, peeled and cut
   into thin matchsticks (350 g)
1 teaspoon sugar, extra
1 tablespoon white vinegar,
   extra

➤ PEEL CUCUMBER and slice in half, horizontally.
1 Scoop out cucumber seeds; slice flesh into thin sticks. Combine with salt in a bowl and stand 30 minutes. Combine onion, vinegar, water, sugar and half the extra salt in another bowl. Stand 1 hour.

2 Combine carrots, remaining salt, sugar and vinegar in a third bowl; stand 30 minutes. Rinse cucumber well and add to the bowl with the onions. Mix well. Stand 1 hour.
3 Combine all vegetables in one serving bowl. Stand another 15 minutes. Serve as a sweet-tart accompaniment to grilled meat.

COOK'S FILE

Storage time: Unused marinated vegetables can be kept for several weeks in a sealed container in the refrigerator. Make sure the vegetables are covered by the marinade.

SCALLOPED POTATO AND TOMATO GRATIN

Preparation time: 15 minutes
Total cooking time: 1 hour 15 minutes
Serves 8

8 medium potatoes (1.5 kg)
45 g butter, melted
1 tablespoon chopped fresh
   herbs (such as thyme,
   marjoram, parsley, rosemary
   and oregano)
1/2 teaspoon cracked black
   pepper
1/2 teaspoon salt
1 1/4 cups cream

2 medium ripe tomatoes
1/2 cup fresh breadcrumbs
1 cup grated cheddar cheese
1 tablespoon chopped chives

➤ PREHEAT OVEN to moderate 180°C.
1 Peel and thinly slice the potatoes. Brush the inside of a shallow baking or pie dish with butter, and arrange the potatoes in a circle so that they overlap.
2 Scatter on the herbs, pepper and salt and pour the cream into the centre of the dish. Cover with foil, bake 1 hour. (At this point the dish can be removed from the oven, allowed to cool, then refrigerated for later.)

Increase oven to moderately hot 210°C (190°C gas) and remove from oven.
3 Thinly slice tomatoes. Remove foil and arrange tomatoes over potato. Scatter evenly with combined crumbs and cheese and return to the oven. Bake, uncovered, 15 minutes until top turns golden. Sprinkle with chives. Serve immediately.

COOK'S FILE

Storage time: Potatoes with herbs and cream can be cooked ahead, then reheated in a microwave or in a low oven. Add tomatoes and topping and bake just before serving
Variation: Thinly slice a medium onion. Layer alternately with potato.

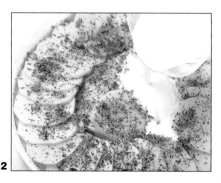

Marinated Onion, Cucumber and Carrot Salad (top)
Scalloped Potato and Tomato Gratin.

CURLY ENDIVE SALAD WITH CRISP PROSCIUTTO AND GARLIC CROÛTONS

Preparation time: 20 minutes
Total cooking time: Nil
Serves 4–6

1 large bunch curly endive
1/2 red oak leaf lettuce
2 red onions
4 slices white or
    brown bread
2 large cloves garlic, crushed
50 g butter, softened
35 g feta cheese, mashed
4–6 thin slices prosciutto ham
1 large avocado

Dressing
2 tablespoons olive oil
1/4 cup sugar
1/4 cup spicy tomato sauce
1 tablespoon soy sauce
1/3 cup red wine vinegar

➤ RINSE ENDIVE and oak leaf lettuce in cold water. Shake lightly in tea-towel to absorb excess water. Tear endive and lettuce into pieces.

1 Peel and slice onions; separate into rings. Combine endive, lettuce and onions in salad bowl or wide shallow dish.

2 Toast bread one side only. Mash garlic, butter and feta cheese into a paste, spread over the untoasted side of the bread. Remove crusts; toast buttered side of bread until crisp and golden on the surface. Cut each slice into 1 cm cubes.

3 Place prosciutto under very hot grill for a few seconds until crisp. Remove and cut into 5 cm pieces. Set aside. Cut avocado into thin wedges.

4 To make Dressing: Whisk oil, sugar, tomato sauce, soy sauce and vinegar together in small bowl.
Add prosciutto and avocado to the salad and pour over half the dressing. Arrange croûtons on top and serve remaining dressing in a jug.

COOK'S FILE

Storage time: Dressing can be prepared 1 day in advance, but salad must be assembled and dressed just before serving.

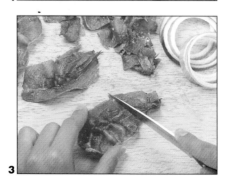

CHICKPEA SALAD

Preparation time: 20 minutes
Total cooking time: Nil or 2 hours 30 minutes (if using dried peas)
Serves 6–8

1³/4 cups (370 g) dried chickpeas, or 2 large cans chickpeas
3¹/2 litres water
¹/4 cup olive oil
1 medium red onion
3 medium tomatoes
1 small red capsicum
4 spring onions
1 cup chopped fresh parsley
2–3 tablespoons chopped fresh mint leaves

Dressing
2 tablespoons tahini (sesame paste)
2 tablespoons fresh lemon juice
2 tablespoons water
¹/4 cup olive oil
2 cloves garlic, crushed
¹/2 teaspoon ground cumin
salt and pepper, to taste

➤ IF USING dried chickpeas, place in medium pan. Cover with water and oil. Bring to the boil, partially cover and cook on medium heat 2¹/2 hours or until tender. (Chickpeas will cook in about 30 minutes in a pressure cooker.)

1 Pour chickpeas into colander. Rinse thoroughly with cold water and set aside to drain. If using canned chickpeas, drain well, rinse and drain again.

2 Peel the onion; slice thinly. Cut tomatoes in half; remove seeds with a spoon. Cut tomato flesh into small pieces. Slice capsicum and spring onions into long thin strips. Combine onion, tomatoes, capsicum and spring onion in a bowl. Add the cooled chickpeas, parsley and mint.

3 To make Dressing: Combine tahini, juice, water, oil, garlic, cumin, salt and pepper in a screwtop jar and shake vigorously to make a creamy liquid. Pour over the salad; mix through.

COOK'S FILE

Storage: Salad can be made several hours before serving. Store, covered, in refrigerator.

ASIAN NOODLE VEGETABLE SALAD

Preparation time: 30 minutes
Total cooking time: 15 minutes
Serves 4–6

6 spring onions
500 g thick rice (or egg) noodles
4 ripe plum tomatoes
1 medium carrot
12 snow peas
120 g can baby corn, drained and halved (or fresh)
150 g fresh bean sprouts
1/4 cup (40 g) roasted peanuts

Dressing
2 teaspoons sesame oil
1/4 cup olive oil
5 teaspoons white rice vinegar
1 1/4 teaspoons sugar
salt and cracked black pepper, to taste
1 teaspoon finely chopped fresh red chilli
1–2 tablespoons chopped fresh coriander

➤ TRIM SPRING ONIONS, cut in thin diagonal slices.

1 Cook noodles in large pan of boiling water 3–4 minutes or until just tender. Remove from heat, drain. Rinse under cold water and drain again.

2 Mark a cross on the top of each tomato. Place in boiling water 1–2 minutes; plunge into cold water; drain. Peel down skin at cross. Cut tomatoes in half, remove seeds. Cut flesh into narrow strips. Peel carrot, cut into thin matchstick lengths. Trim snow peas, cut into diagonal slices. If using fresh baby corn, boil in lightly salted water 3 minutes; drain. Plunge in cold water; drain and set aside. Plunge bean sprouts into boiling water 1–2 minutes; drain. Combine all vegetables and peanuts in a salad bowl. Add Dressing and mix thoroughly. Chill briefly before serving. Drizzle with soy sauce, if desired.

3 To make Dressing: Combine oils, vinegar, sugar, salt, pepper, chilli and coriander in a screwtop jar; shake vigorously to combine.

C O O K ' S   F I L E

Storage time: Salad is best made just before serving. Dressing will keep in refrigerator 1 week; store in a screwtop jar.

BARBECUED CORN ON THE COB WITH TOMATO RELISH

Preparation time: 15 minutes
Total cooking time: 1 hour
Serves 6

Tomato Relish
400 g can peeled tomatoes
2/3 cup white vinegar
1/2 cup white sugar
1 clove garlic, finely chopped
2 spring onions, finely chopped
4 sun-dried tomatoes, finely chopped
1 small fresh red chilli, finely chopped

1/2 teaspoon salt
cracked black pepper to taste

6 large cobs fresh corn
1–2 tablespoons olive or vegetable oil
60 g butter
salt to taste

➤ PREPARE AND HEAT barbecue.
1 To make Tomato Relish: Roughly chop tomatoes or process briefly in a food processor bowl. Combine vinegar and sugar in medium pan. Stir over medium heat until sugar dissolves. Bring to boil. Reduce heat and simmer 2 minutes; add tomatoes, garlic, spring onions, sun-dried tomatoes and chilli. Bring to the boil, reduce heat and simmer 35 minutes, stirring frequently.

2 Add salt and pepper and continue to cook until relish has thickened. Remove from the heat and allow to cool.
3 Brush the corn with oil and cook on the hot lightly greased barbecue grill 5 minutes, each side, until corn is soft and cobs are flecked with brown in places. Using tongs, lift the corn onto the flatplate and moisten each with a square of butter. Sprinkle with salt. Serve at once with Tomato Relish.

COOK'S FILE

Storage time: Corn is best cooked just before serving. Relish will keep several weeks in the refrigerator, stored in an airtight container.
Note: Serve relish as a spicy accompaniment to cornbread and cheese, or with barbecued sausages.

BARBECUED MUSHROOMS

Preparation time: 10 minutes
Total cooking time: 5 minutes
Serves 6

6 large mushrooms
50 g butter, melted
2 cloves garlic, crushed
2 tablespoons finely chopped
   fresh chives
1 tablespoon fresh thyme leaves
1/2 cup shredded parmesan
   cheese

➤ PREPARE AND HEAT barbecue.
1 Carefully peel skin from mushroom caps. Remove stalks. Combine butter and garlic in a small bowl.
2 Brush tops of mushrooms with garlic butter, place top-side down on hot barbecue flatplate and cook over the hottest part of the fire 2 minutes or until tops have browned. Turn mushrooms over. Brush upturned bases with garlic butter; cook 2 minutes.
3 Sprinkle bases with combined chives and thyme, then cheese, and cook a further 3 minutes, until cheese begins to melt. Serve immediately.

COOK'S FILE

Storage time: Mushrooms are best cooked just before serving.
Hint: Mushrooms can also be cooked in a heavy-based frying pan. Lightly grease the pan with butter and cook 2–3 minutes either side. Add fresh herbs and cheese, then place pan under hot preheated grill until cheese has melted.
Any type of mushroom can be used in this recipe. Larger types such as flat or field mushrooms will take longer to cook than button or cup. Mushrooms should remain firm and chewy after cooking.

CHINESE VEGETABLE STIR-FRY

Preparation time: 20 minutes
Total cooking time: 6 minutes
Serves 4–6

1 medium red capsicum
100 g oyster mushrooms
425 g can baby corn
500 g Chinese cabbage
1 tablespoon olive oil
250 g fresh bean sprouts
5 spring onions, cut into 3 cm
   pieces
2 cloves garlic, crushed
1 tablespoon olive oil

2 teaspoons sesame oil
2 tablespoons teriyaki marinade
1/2 teaspoon sugar
sweet chilli sauce, to taste

➤ PREPARE AND HEAT barbecue. Cut capsicum in half, remove seeds and membrane. Cut into thin strips. Slice mushrooms in half. Cut any large baby corn in half.
1 Cut cabbage into thick slices, then crosswise into squares.
2 Brush barbecue flatplate with oil. Stir-fry capsicum, mushrooms, corn, cabbage, sprouts, spring onions and garlic 4 minutes, tossing and stirring to prevent burning or sticking.
3 Pour over combined olive oil,

sesame oil, teriyaki marinade and sugar, stir thoroughly to coat and cook 1 minute longer. Serve immediately. Drizzle with sweet chilli sauce.

COOK'S FILE

Storage time: Vegetables must be cooked just before serving.
Note: Teriyaki marinade is available from most supermarkets. Oyster mushrooms and Chinese cabbage are available from some greengrocers and most Asian food shops. If unavailable, or if preferred, substitute other vegetables such as, zucchini, broccoli, cauliflower, green beans, onions or carrot. All ingredients should be about the same size to ensure even cooking.

Barbecued Mushrooms (top)
and Chinese Vegetable Stir-fry.

RED POTATO SALAD

Preparation time: 20 minutes
Total cooking time: 10 minutes
Serves 8

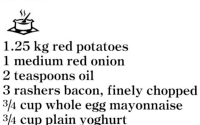

1.25 kg red potatoes
1 medium red onion
2 teaspoons oil
3 rashers bacon, finely chopped
3/4 cup whole egg mayonnaise
3/4 cup plain yoghurt
3 spring onions, finely chopped

➤ SCRUB POTATOES thoroughly and cut into 3 cm pieces.

1 Cook potatoes in large pan of boiling water 5 minutes or until just tender. Drain and cool completely. Cut onion in half and slice finely. Heat oil in frying pan. Cook bacon 5 minutes or until well browned and crisp. Drain on paper towel.

2 Place potatoes, bacon and onion in a large mixing bowl. Combine mayonnaise, yoghurt and spring onions in a small mixing bowl, pour over potato mixture.

3 Fold through gently, taking care not to break up potatoes. Transfer to a large serving bowl and serve at room temperature.

COOK'S FILE

Storage time: Potato salad can be made up to 1 day in advance. Store, covered, in the refrigerator, allowing salad to return to room temperature before serving.

Note: Do not peel potatoes; the skin provides colour and texture in the salad. Potatoes should be well scrubbed and thoroughly dried before use.

Variation: Use whole baby potatoes in this salad. Cook approximately twice as long as potato pieces.

1

2

3

MIXED HERB TABOULI

Preparation time: 20 minutes
Total cooking time: Nil
Serves 8

3/4 cup burghul
3/4 cup hot water
2 bunches continental (flat-leaf)
    parsley
1 bunch chives
1 1/2 cups fresh basil leaves

1/2 cup fresh mint leaves
4 spring onions, finely chopped
3 medium tomatoes, chopped
1/3 cup lemon juice
1/4 cup olive oil

➤ COMBINE BURGHUL and hot water in medium bowl.

1 Stand 15 minutes or until all the water has been absorbed.

2 Remove large stalks from parsley and discard. Wash and dry other herbs thoroughly. Chop well with a large, sharp knife or in food processor. (If using a food processor, take care not to over-process.)

3 Place burghul, parsley, chives, basil, mint, spring onions, tomatoes, juice and oil in serving bowl and toss well to combine. Refrigerate until required.

COOK'S FILE

Storage time: Tabouli can be made up to 4 hours ahead.
Note: Burghul is a cracked wheat, available in health food shops.

TRI-COLOUR PASTA SALAD

Preparation time: 20 minutes
Total cooking time: 10 minutes
Serves 6

2 tablespoons olive oil
2 tablespoons white wine
    vinegar
1 small garlic clove, halved
375 g tri-colour pasta spirals
1 tablespoon olive oil, extra
³/4 cup sun-dried tomatoes in oil,
    drained

¹/2 cup black pitted olives
100 g parmesan cheese
1 cup quartered artichoke
    hearts
¹/2 cup shredded fresh basil
    leaves

➤ COMBINE OLIVE OIL, vinegar
and garlic in a small screwtop jar.
Shake well to mix and allow to stand
1 hour.
1 Cook pasta in a large pan of boiling
water until just tender. Drain and toss
with extra olive oil while still hot. Cool
completely.
2 Cut sun-dried tomatoes into fine

strips and cut olives in half. Cut
parmesan cheese into paper-thin slices.
3 Place pasta, tomatoes, olives,
cheese, artichokes and basil in a large
serving bowl. Pour dressing over,
remove garlic pieces, and toss to combine. Serve immediately.

COOK'S FILE

Storage time: Salad can be assembled up to 4 hours in advance.
Refrigerate until required; allow to
come to room temperature. Add
cheese and basil just before serving.
Hint: Serve this salad with barbecued
steak or roast chicken.

1

2

3

WILD AND BROWN RICE SALAD

Preparation time: 10 minutes
Total cooking time: 1 hour 15 minutes
Serves 6–8

1 cup brown rice
¹/₂ cup wild rice
1 medium red onion
1 small red capsicum
2 sticks celery
2 tablespoons chopped
parsley
¹/₃ cup chopped pecans

Dressing
¹/₄ **cup orange juice**
¹/₄ **cup lemon juice**
1 **teaspoon finely grated orange**
rind
1 **teaspoon finely grated lemon**
rind
¹/₃ **cup olive oil**

➤ COOK BROWN RICE in a pan of boiling water 25–30 minutes until just tender. Drain well and cool completely. Boil wild rice 30–40 minutes; drain well and cool.

1 Chop onion and capsicum finely. Cut celery into thin slices. Combine in bowl with parsley and cooked rices. Place pecans in a dry frying pan and stir over medium heat 2–3 minutes until lightly toasted. Transfer to plate to cool.

2 To make Dressing: Place juices, rinds and oil in a small screwtop jar; shake well to combine.

3 Pour dressing over salad and fold through. Add pecans and gently mix through. Serve with bread, if desired.

COOK'S FILE

Storage time: Salad can be assembled up to 4 hours in advance.

SNOW PEA SALAD

Preparation time: 10 minutes
Total cooking time: Nil
Serves 6–8

150 g snow peas
1 bunch fresh asparagus
2 medium carrots, peeled
425 g can baby corn, drained
230 g can bamboo shoots,
    drained

Dressing
1/4 cup vegetable oil
3 teaspoons sesame oil
1 tablespoon soy sauce

➤ TRIM SNOW PEAS; cut in half.
1 Remove woody ends from asparagus and cut into 5 cm lengths. Cut carrots into matchsticks.
2 Place snow peas and asparagus in a heatproof bowl and cover with boiling water. Stand 1 minute, drain and plunge into iced water. Drain and dry thoroughly on paper towels.
3 Combine snow peas, asparagus, carrots, corn and bamboo shoots in serving bowl. Pour on Dressing. Serve with garlic bread, if desired.
To make Dressing: Place oils and sauce in a small screwtop jar; shake well to combine.

COOK'S FILE

Storage time: Salad is best made just before serving.
Note: Sesame oil is a very strongly flavoured oil used in many Asian dishes. It should be used sparingly as its flavour tends to dominate. Sesame oil comes in different strengths, and the darker the oil the stronger the flavour. It is available in the Asian food section of the supermarket or Asian supermarkets.

BABY BARBECUED POTATOES

Preparation time: 20 minutes
+ 1 hour standing
Total cooking time: 20 minutes
Serves 6

750 g baby potatoes
2 tablespoons olive oil
2 tablespoons fresh thyme
  leaves
2 teaspoons crushed sea salt

➤ WASH POTATOES thoroughly under cold water. Cut any large potatoes in half so that all potatoes are a uniform size for even cooking.

1 Boil, steam or microwave potatoes until just tender. (Potatoes should remain whole and intact.) Drain and lightly dry with paper towels.

2 Place potatoes in large mixing bowl; add oil and thyme. Toss gently to coat potatoes, stand 1 hour. Prepare and heat barbecue.

3 Place potatoes on hot, lightly greased barbecue flatplate. Cook

15 minutes, turning frequently and brushing with remaining oil and thyme mixture, until golden brown. Place in serving bowl and sprinkle with salt. Garnish with extra thyme sprigs, if desired.

COOK'S FILE

Storage time: Potatoes can be cooked and marinated 2 hours in advance. Barbecue just before serving.
Note: Sea salt is a pure form of salt that comes in large crystals. Table salt can be substituted.

WEBER/ KETTLE COOKERY

ORANGE AND GINGER GLAZED HAM

Preparation time: 25 minutes
Total cooking time: 1 hour 30 minutes
Serves 20

6 kg ham on the bone
$^{1}/4$ cup orange juice
$^{3}/4$ cup orange marmalade
1 tablespoon grated ginger
2 teaspoons mustard powder
2 tablespoons soft brown sugar
whole cloves (about 30)

➤ PREPARE WEBER (kettle) barbecue for indirect cooking at moderate heat (normal fire).
1 Remove rind by running your thumb around edge of ham, under the rind. Begin pulling from the widest edge. When rind has been removed to within 10 cm of the shank end, cut through the rind around the shank. Using a sharp knife, remove excess fat from ham; discard fat. (Reserve rind for crackling, if desired. Rub rind with salt and barbecue for 40 minutes.)

2 Using a sharp knife score top of ham with deep diagonal cuts. Score diagonally the other way, forming a diamond pattern. Place ham on barbecue; put lid on barbecue and cook 45 minutes.
3 Place juice, marmalade, ginger, mustard and sugar in small pan. Stir over medium heat until combined; set aside to cool. Remove lid from barbecue; carefully press cloves into top of ham (approximately one clove per diamond); brush all over with marmalade mixture. Cover barbecue, cook a further 45 minutes. Serve garnished with clove-studded orange slices, if desired. Ham can be served warm or cold.

COOK'S FILE

Storage time: Cover ham with a clean, dry cloth; store in refrigerator up to 1 month. Change the cloth every 2–3 days.
Note: Leftover ham can be sliced and served with fried eggs, or with grilled tomatoes. Cubed ham is delicious in fried rice. The ham bone can be used for stock or as the basis of pea soup.

WHOLE FILLET OF BEEF WITH MUSTARD COATING

Preparation time: 1 hour 5 minutes
  + 15 minutes standing
Total cooking time: 40 minutes
Serves 6–8

2 kg scotch fillet of beef
1/4 cup brandy

Mustard Coating
1/3 cup wholegrain mustard
1/4 cup cream
3/4 teaspoon black pepper,
  coarsely ground

➤ PREPARE WEBER (kettle) barbecue for indirect cooking at moderate heat (normal fire). Trim meat of excess fat and sinew.

1 Tie meat securely with string at regular intervals to retain its shape. Brush beef all over with the brandy; stand 1 hour.

2 To make Mustard Coating: Combine mustard, cream and pepper in small bowl. Spread evenly over top and sides of fillet.

3 Place meat on large greased sheet of foil. Grasp corners of foil and pinch securely to form a tray. (This will hold in the juices.) Place lid on barbecue and cook 30–40 minutes for medium-rare meat. Stand 10–15 minutes before carving into thick slices. Serve warm with barbecued or grilled vegetables.

COOK'S FILE

Storage time: Beef can be marinated in brandy up to 1 day in advance. Store, covered, in refrigerator.

Hint: Reserve cooking juices left in foil to make a gravy; stir in a tablespoon of prepared mustard.

WEBER CHICKEN

Preparation time: 10 minutes
Total cooking time: 1 hour 30 minutes
Serves 4–6

1.8 kg chicken
salt
1/2 teaspoon cracked
    peppercorns
1 whole head garlic
small bunch fresh oregano
1/4 cup olive oil

➤ PREPARE WEBER (kettle) barbecue) for indirect cooking at medium heat (normal fire). Place a drip tray underneath top grill. Remove giblets and any large fat deposits from chicken. Wipe chicken and pat dry with paper towel. Season chicken cavity with salt and pepper.

1 Using a sharp knife, cut off top of head of garlic. Push the whole head of garlic, unpeeled, into the cavity. Follow with whole bunch of oregano. Close cavity with several toothpicks or a skewer.

2 Rub chicken skin with salt and brush with oil. Place on barbecue over drip tray. Put lid on barbecue and cook 1 hour, brushing occasionally with olive oil to keep the skin moist. Insert skewer into chicken thigh. If juices run clear chicken is cooked through. Stand chicken away from heat 5 minutes before carving.

3 Carefully separate garlic cloves; serve 1 or 2 cloves with each serving of chicken. (The flesh can be squeezed from the clove and eaten with chicken, according to taste.)

1

2

3

SPICED SWEET POTATOES

Preparation time: 20 minutes
Total cooking time: 25 minutes
Serves 4–6

500 g orange sweet potatoes
¼ cup demerara sugar
¾ teaspoon mixed spice

30 g butter, chopped
⅓ cup orange juice

➤ PREPARE WEBER (kettle) barbecue for indirect cooking at moderate heat (normal fire). Peel sweet potatoes and cut into thick slices.

1 Arrange in layers in shallow greased tray. Sprinkle over combined sugar and mixed spice; dot with butter.
2 Sprinkle over the orange juice.

3 Cover tray with foil, place on top grill of barbecue, replace lid, cook 20 minutes. Remove foil and test with a sharp knife; cook a few more minutes, if necessary. Sprinkle over a little more orange juice if potatoes begin to dry out.

COOK'S FILE

Storage time: This dish is best cooked just before serving.

BARBECUED LAMB SHANKS

Preparation time: 5 minutes
  + overnight marinating ·
Total cooking time: 45 minutes
Serves 6

2 cloves garlic, halved
1/3 cup olive oil
6 lamb shanks
salt and pepper, to taste

➤ COMBINE GARLIC and oil in small bowl, cover and marinate, at room temperature, overnight.

1 Prepare weber (kettle) barbecue for indirect cooking at moderate heat (normal fire). Place drip tray under top grill. Trim shanks of excess fat and sinew.

2 Brush the garlic oil generously over the shanks and sprinkle with salt and pepper.

3 Place lamb shanks on the top grill of the barbecue, cover with lid and roast 35–45 minutes or until the meat is tender when pierced with a fork. Serve with barbecued vegetables, such as capsicum, and thick slices of chargrilled potato, scattered with herbs, if desired.

COOK'S FILE

Storage time: Lamb shanks can be marinated and stored in refrigerator 1 day in advance.

Hint: For a more intense flavour, double the quantity of garlic in the oil and brush over lamb several hours before cooking. Pour remaining garlic oil over shanks before serving.

Variation: Try this recipe with other boned cuts of meat, such as lamb neck chops, osso bucco, pieces of ox tail and chicken drumsticks.

1

2

3

LEG OF LAMB

Preparation time: 15 minutes
Total cooking time: 1 hour 30 minutes
Serves 6

2 kg leg of lamb
4 cloves garlic
6–8 sprigs rosemary
2 tablespoons olive oil
2 tablespoons freshly ground
    black pepper

➤ PREPARE WEBER (kettle) barbecue for indirect cooking at moderate heat (normal fire). Place a drip tray on the bottom grill.

1 Trim meat of excess fat and sinew. Cut narrow, deep slits all over top and sides of meat.

2 Cut garlic cloves in half lengthways. Push garlic and rosemary sprigs into slits. Brush all over with oil and sprinkle with black pepper.

3 Place lamb on barbecue grill over drip tray, cover and cook 1 hour 30 minutes for medium-rare meat. Brush with olive oil occasionally. Stand lamb in a warm place, covered with foil, 10–15 minutes before carving.

COOK'S FILE

Storage time: Barbecue lamb just before serving.
Variation: A pump leg of lamb (pickled lamb) can be used in this recipe. Pump lamb is available through specialty butchers.

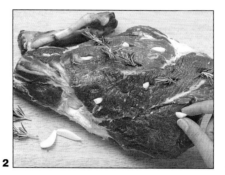

BAKED VEGETABLES

Preparation time: 20 minutes
Total cooking time: 1 hour 15 minutes
Serves 6

6 medium potatoes
60 g butter, melted
1/4 teaspoon paprika
750 g pumpkin
6 small onions
150 g green beans
150 g broccoli
20 g butter, chopped, extra

➤ PREPARE WEBER (kettle) barbecue for indirect cooking at moderate heat (normal fire). Peel potatoes and cut in half.

1 Using a small, sharp knife, make deep, fine cuts into potato, taking care not to cut all the way through. Take two large sheets of aluminium foil, fold in half and brush liberally with some melted butter. Place potatoes unscored-side down on foil and fold up edges of foil to create a tray. Brush potatoes generously with melted butter and sprinkle with paprika.

2 Cut pumpkin into three wedges, cut each wedge in half. Peel onions and trim bases slightly, so they will sit flat on grill. Brush pumpkin and onions with melted butter. Place tray of potatoes, pumpkin pieces and onions on barbecue grill. Put lid on barbecue; cook 1 hour.

3 Top and tail beans; cut broccoli into florets. Place on a sheet of foil brushed with melted butter. Dot with extra butter; enclose completely in foil. Add to other vegetables on grill, cook a further 15 minutes.

COOK'S FILE

Storage time: Vegetables are best cooked before serving.
Hint: If barbecuing a chicken or leg of lamb, cook vegetables simultneously, timing them to be ready with the meat. If vegetables are cooked early, store, wrapped in foil, in a warm place until needed.
Variation: Use any of your favourite vegetables for this recipe. Hard vegetables, such as turnips and sweet potatoes can be placed directly on the grill. Smaller or leafier vegetables, such as mushrooms, spinach or asparagus, can be cooked in foil parcels. Cooking times are the same as for a conventional oven.

Leg of Lamb
with Baked Vegetables.

SMOKED CHICKEN FILLETS

Preparation time: 5 minutes
Total cooking time: 25 minutes
Serves 4

4 chicken breast
    fillets (1 kg)
1 tablespoon olive oil

seasoned pepper, to taste
hickory or mesquite chips, for
    smoking

➤ PREPARE WEBER (kettle) barbecue for indirect cooking at moderate heat (normal fire). Trim chicken of excess fat and sinew.
1 Brush chicken with oil and sprinkle over the seasoned pepper.
2 Spoon a pile of smoking chips (about 25) over the coals in each charcoal rail.
3 Cover barbecue and cook chicken 15 minutes. Test with a sharp knife. If juices do not run clear cook another 5–10 minutes until cooked as desired. Serve with chilli noodles, if liked.

COOK'S FILE

Storage time: Chicken is best smoked just before serving.

1

2

3

WHOLE FISH WITH LEMON HERB BUTTER

Preparation time: 15 minutes
Total cooking time: 1 hour
Serves 4

2 kg whole white-fleshed fish

Herb Butter
**80 g butter, softened
1 tablespoon chopped parsley
3 teaspoons thyme leaves
1 tablespoon chopped chives
2 teaspoons grated lemon rind**

1 small lemon, sliced

➤ PREPARE WEBER (kettle) barbe-cue for indirect cooking at moderate heat (normal fire).
1 Wash and scale fish; pat dry with a paper towel. Place fish on a large sheet of oiled aluminium foil.
2 To make Herb Butter: Blend butter, herbs and lemon rind in a small bowl; beat until smooth. Spread half of the butter mixture inside the cavity of the fish. Transfer the remaining butter mixture to a serving bowl.
3 Lay lemon slices over the fish, enclose fish in foil and place on barbe-cue grill. Cover, cook 1 hour or until flesh flakes back easily with a fork. Serve with extra Herb Butter.

COOK'S FILE

Storage time: Herb Butter can be made up to 2 weeks in advance, pro-vided it is well covered and refrigerated. Fish is best cooked just before serving.
Note: Leftover Herb Butter can be spread on hot bread, or served with cooked vegetables or meats such as steak and chicken.

FINISHING TOUCHES

OLIVE DAMPER

Preparation time: 20 minutes
Total cooking time: 25 minutes
Serves 8

2 cups self-raising flour
1 teaspoon salt
30 g butter, chopped
1/2 cup shredded parmesan cheese
1/2 cup black pitted olives, sliced
1 tablespoon chopped fresh
   rosemary
1/2 cup milk
1/4 cup water
1 tablespoon milk, extra
2 tablespoons shredded
   parmesan cheese, extra

➤ PREHEAT OVEN to moderately hot 210°C (190°C gas).
1 Brush a baking tray with melted butter or oil, and sprinkle lightly with flour. Sift self-raising flour and salt into mixing bowl. Add chopped butter. Using fingertips, rub butter into flour until mixture is fine and crumbly.
2 Add parmesan, olives and rosemary; stir. Combine milk and water; add to dry ingredients. Mix to a soft dough with flat-bladed knife.
3 Turn out onto a lightly floured surface, knead briefly until smooth. Shape into a ball, flatten out to a 2 cm thick round.
4 Place dough on prepared baking tray. Using a large knife, score dough deeply into eight portions. Brush with extra milk and sprinkle with extra cheese. Bake 25 minutes or until golden brown and crusty.

COOK'S FILE

Storage time: Damper is most delicious served straight from the oven.

GARLIC FOCACCIA

Preparation time: 20 minutes
  + 50 minutes proving
Total cooking time: 25 minutes
Serves 4–6

7 g sachet dry yeast
1 teaspoon sugar
1 teaspoon plain flour
3/4 cup lukewarm water
2¹/3 cups plain flour, extra
1 teaspoon salt
3 cloves garlic, crushed
2 tablespoons olive oil
1 tablespoon cornmeal or
  semolina
1 tablespoon olive oil, extra
2 teaspoons finely crushed sea
  salt

➤ COMBINE YEAST, sugar, flour
and water in small mixing bowl.
1 Stand, covered with plastic wrap, in
a warm place 10 minutes or until
foamy.
2 Sift extra flour and salt into a large
mixing bowl. Add garlic and stir with
a knife to combine. Make a well in the
centre, stir in yeast mixture and olive
oil. Using a flat-bladed knife, mix to a
firm dough.
3 Turn dough onto lightly floured
surface, knead for 10 minutes. Shape
dough into a ball, place in a large,
lightly oiled mixing bowl. Stand,
covered with plastic wrap, in a
warm place 40 minutes or until
well risen.
4 Preheat oven to moderately hot
210°C (190°C gas). Sprinkle the base of
an 18 x 28 cm shallow tin with cornmeal or semolina. Knead dough again
2 minutes or until smooth. Press
dough into tin; prick deep holes with a
skewer. Sprinkle lightly with water
and place in oven. Bake 10 minutes,
sprinkle again with water. Bake a further 10 minutes, brush with extra
olive oil, sprinkle with sea salt, then
bake 5 more minutes. Serve warm or
at room temperature, cut into squares.

COOK'S FILE

Storage time: Focaccia is best made
on the day of serving.
Variation: Add herbs or olives to the
dough, if desired. Use table salt
instead of sea salt, if preferred.

CREAMY LIME TART

Preparation time: 30 minutes
    + 20 minutes refrigeration
Total cooking time: 1 hour 5 minutes
Serves 12

1¼ cups plain flour
½ cup ground almonds
90 g butter, chopped
1–2 tablespoons iced water

Filling
6 egg yolks
½ cup caster sugar
100 g butter, melted
⅓ cup lime juice
2 teaspoons finely grated lime rind
2 teaspoons gelatine
1 tablespoon water, extra
½ cup cream, whipped
½ cup sugar
¼ cup water
rind of 4 limes, finely shredded

➤ PREHEAT OVEN to moderate 180°C.
1 Sift flour into a large mixing bowl, add almonds and chopped butter. Using fingertips, rub butter into flour 2 minutes or until mixture is fine and crumbly. Add almost all the water, mix to a firm dough, adding more liquid if necessary. Turn pastry onto a lightly floured surface, press together until smooth. Roll pastry out to fit a 23 cm fluted flan tin. Line tin with pastry, trim edges and refrigerate 20 minutes. Cut a sheet of greaseproof paper large enough to cover pastry-lined tin. Spread a layer of dried beans or rice evenly over paper. Bake 20 minutes. Remove from oven; discard paper and rice. Return pastry to oven for a further 20 minutes or until lightly golden. Cool completely.
2 To make Filling: Place egg yolks, sugar, butter, lime juice and rind in a medium heatproof bowl. Whisk to combine thoroughly and dissolve sugar. Stand bowl over a pan of simmering water and stir constantly 15 minutes until mixture thickens. Remove from heat and cool slightly. Combine gelatine with water in a small bowl. Stand bowl in hot water; stir until dissolved. Add gelatine mixture to lime curd, stir to combine thoroughly. Cool to room temperature, stirring occasionally.
3 Fold whipped cream through lime curd; pour into pastry case. Refrigerate 2–3 hours until set; stand 15 minutes at room temperature before serving. Decorate with glazed lime rind.
To prepare glazed lime rind: Combine sugar and extra water in a small pan. Stir without boiling until sugar has completely dissolved. Bring to the boil, add lime rind and simmer 3 minutes. Remove rind from pan, lay on wire rack to drain.

COOK'S FILE

Storage time: Tart can be prepared up to 4 hours in advance.

1

2

3

PAVLOVA

Preparation time: 15 minutes
Total cooking time: 40 minutes
Serves 6–8

6 egg whites
1½ cups caster sugar
1 cup cream, whipped
125 g strawberries,
    hulled and halved
2 kiwi fruit, peeled
    and sliced

1 banana, sliced
pulp of 2 passionfruit

➤PREHEAT OVEN to slow 150°C.
Line a tray with baking paper. Mark a
22 cm circle on paper.
1 Place egg whites in bowl, beat with
electric beaters until soft peaks form.
Gradually add sugar, beating well
after each addition. Beat several minutes until sugar has dissolved and
meringue is thick and glossy.
2 Spoon meringue mixture onto tray.
Spread over tray, using the circle as a

guide. Smooth edge and top with flat-
bladed knife.
3 Bake in oven 40 minutes or until
pale and crisp. Turn off oven, cool
meringue in oven, leaving door ajar.
Just before serving, spread with cream
and top with strawberries, kiwi fruit,
banana and passionfruit pulp.

COOK'S FILE

Storage time: Pavlova can be made
1 day ahead and stored in an airtight
container. Top with cream and fruit
just before serving.

1

2

3

FRUIT KEBABS WITH HONEY CARDAMOM SYRUP

Preparation time: 15 minutes
+ 1 hour marinating
Total cooking time: 5 minutes
Makes 8 kebabs

1/4 small pineapple, peeled
1 peach
1 banana, peeled
16 strawberries

Honey Cardamom Syrup
2 tablespoons honey
20 g butter, melted
1/2 teaspoon ground cardamom
1 tablespoon rum or brandy
1 tablespoon soft brown sugar

➤CUT PINEAPPLE into eight bite-sized pieces.

1 Cut peach into 8 wedges and slice banana. Thread all fruit alternately on skewers; place in shallow dish.

2 To make Honey Cardamom Syrup: Combine honey, butter, cardamom, rum and sugar in bowl. Pour mixture over kebabs, brush to coat. Cover; stand at room temperature 1 hour. Prepare and heat barbecue.

3 Cook kebabs on hot lightly greased barbecue flatplate 5 minutes. Brush with syrup while cooking. Serve drizzled with remaining syrup. Top with a dollop of fresh cream or yoghurt, if desired.

COOK'S FILE

Storage time: Kebabs best cooked just before serving.

GINGER PEAR CHEESECAKE

Preparation time: 25 minutes
+ 3 hours refrigeration
Total cooking time: 2 minutes
Serves 8

250 g gingersnap biscuits
2 tablespoons caster sugar
125 g butter, melted

Filling
1/4 cup water
1 tablespoon gelatine
375 g cream cheese
1/3 cup caster sugar
1 tablespoon lemon juice

1 cup cream, whipped
425 g can pear halves, drained
   and sliced
2 tablespoons chopped glacé
   ginger

➤ BRUSH A 20 cm springform tin
with melted butter or oil.
1 Place biscuits in food processor
bowl and process to form medium
crumbs. Transfer to a mixing bowl,
add sugar and butter, mix well. Press
mixture firmly onto base and sides of
prepared tin. Refrigerate 20 minutes.
2 To make Filling: Combine water
and gelatine in small bowl. Stand in
hot water; stir until dissolved. Cool.
Using electric beaters, beat cream
cheese until softened. Add caster

sugar and beat 3 minutes. Add lemon
juice and beat until combined. Add a
little of this mixture to gelatine, mix
well. Add gelatine to cheese mixture.
3 Using a metal spoon, fold whipped
cream through cheese mixture.
Arrange a layer of pear slices in base
of crust, pour over half the cheese
mixture. Top with another layer of
pears and remaining cheese mixture.
Refrigerate 3 hours or until set.
Decorate outer edge with chopped
glacé ginger.

COOK'S FILE

Storage time: Cheesecake may be
made up to 8 hours in advance.
Variation: Use canned peaches
instead of pears, if preferred.

CHOCOLATE MOUSSE FLAN

Preparation time: 35 minutes
Total cooking time: 5 minutes
Serves 8–10

250 g plain chocolate biscuits,
    finely crushed
125 g butter, melted

Filling
200 g dark cooking chocolate,
    chopped
2 tablespoons cream
2 egg yolks
2 teaspoons gelatine
1 tablespoon water
2/3 cup cream, extra, whipped
2 egg whites

Topping
1 1/2 teaspoons instant coffee
3 teaspoons water
1 cup cream

1 tablespoon caster sugar
cocoa powder, for dusting

➤ BRUSH A 28 cm round fluted flan tin with melted butter or oil. Line base with paper.

1 Combine biscuit crumbs and butter in medium bowl; mix well. Press into base and sides of prepared tin. Refrigerate until firm.

2 To make Filling: Combine chocolate and cream in small pan. Stir over low heat until smooth, remove from heat. Cool slightly, stir in yolks. Sprinkle gelatine over water in small bowl. Stand in boiling water until dissolved. Cool slightly and stir into chocolate mixture. Transfer to medium mixing bowl. Fold whipped cream into chocolate mixture.

3 Beat egg whites in bowl until soft peaks form. Using a metal spoon, fold into chocolate mixture; spread over prepared base. Refrigerate until set. Just before serving, remove from tin and spread with Topping.

4 To make Topping: Dissolve coffee in water; combine with cream and sugar in bowl. Beat until soft peaks form; spread over mousse flan. Dust with sifted cocoa powder just before serving.

COOK'S FILE

Storage time: Mousse flan can be made up to a day ahead. Store, covered, in the refrigerator.

MANGO UPSIDE-DOWN CAKE

Preparation time: 25 minutes
Total cooking time: 55 minutes
Makes one 20 cm cake

2 x 425 g cans sliced mango
60 g butter, melted
2 tablespoons soft brown sugar
3/4 cup self-raising flour
1/4 cup plain flour
1/2 cup ground almonds
185 g butter, extra
1 cup caster sugar
2 eggs, lightly beaten

➤ PREHEAT OVEN to moderate 180°C. Brush a 20 cm tin with melted butter.

1 Drain mango slices and reserve 1/2 cup juice. Combine melted butter and brown sugar, spread over base of tin. Arrange mango slices over sugar mixture.

2 Sift flours into large mixing bowl. Add ground almonds; make a well in the centre. Combine extra butter, caster sugar and reserved juice in medium pan. Stir over low heat until butter has melted and sugar has dissolved; remove from heat. Add the butter mixture to the dry ingredients. Stir with a whisk until just combined. Add eggs; mix well.

3 Pour mixture carefully over mango slices. Bake 55 minutes or until a skewer comes out clean when inserted in centre. Stand cake in tin 5 minutes before turning out onto wire rack to cool. Serve with whipped cream or ice-cream, if desired.

COOK'S FILE

Storage time: Mango Upside-down Cake will keep up to 2 days in an air-tight container.

1

2

3

INDEX

1 cm
2 cm
3 cm
4 cm
5 cm
6 cm
7 cm
8 cm
9 cm
10 cm
11 cm
12 cm
13 cm
14 cm
15 cm
16 cm
17 cm
18 cm
19 cm
20 cm
21 cm
22 cm
23 cm
24 cm
25 cm

USEFUL INFORMATION

All our recipes are tested in the Australian Family Circle® Test Kitchen. Standard metric measuring cups and spoons approved by Standards Australia are used in the development of our recipes. All cup and spoon measurements are level. We have used 60 g (Grade 3) eggs in all recipes. Sizes of cans vary from manufacturer to manufacturer and between countries—use the can size closest to the one suggested in the recipe.

Conversion Guide

1 cup	= 250 ml (8 fl oz)
1 teaspoon	= 5 ml
1 Australian tablespoon	= 20 ml (4 teaspoons)
1 UK/US tablespoon	= 15 ml (3 teaspoons)

NOTE: We have used 20 ml tablespoon measures. If you are using a 15 ml tablespoon, for most recipes the difference will not be noticeable. However, for recipes using baking powder, gelatine, bicarbonate of soda, small amounts of flour and cornflour, add an extra teaspoon for each tablespoon specified.

Dry Measures

30 g	= 1 oz
250 g	= 8 oz
500 g	= 1 lb

Liquid Measures

30 ml	= 1 fl oz
125 ml	= 4 fl oz
250 ml	= 8 fl oz

Linear Measures

6 mm	= ¼ inch
1 cm	= ½ inch
2.5 cm	= 1 inch

Cup Conversions

1 cup cheese, grated, lightly packed:

Cheddar	= 125 g (4 oz)
Parmesan	= 105 g (3½ oz)
Romano	= 125 g (4 oz)
1 cup breadcrumbs, dry	= 105 g (3½ oz)
1 cup breadcrumbs, soft	= 75 g (2½ oz)
1 cup honey	= 345 g (11 oz)
1 cup sugar, granulated	= 250 g (8 oz)
1 cup sugar, soft brown	= 185 g (6 oz)

Oven Temperatures

Cooking times may vary slightly depending on the type of oven you are using. Before you preheat the oven, we suggest that you refer to the manufacturer's instructions to ensure proper temperature control.

	°C	°F	Gas Mark
Very slow	120	250	½
Slow	150	300	2
Warm	170	325	3
Moderate	180	350	4
Mod. hot	190	375	5
Mod. hot	200	400	6
Hot	220	425	7
Very hot	230	450	8

NOTE: For fan-forced ovens check your appliance manual, but as a general rule, set oven temperature to 20°C lower than the temperature indicated in the recipe.

International Glossary

apricot nectar	apricot juice
beef stock powder	beef stock cube
green prawns	raw prawns
sambal oelek	chilli bean paste
Lebanese cucumber	use any cucumber
snow peas	mange toute
orange sweet potato	use sweet potato

Published by Murdoch Books®, a division of Murdoch Magazines Pty Limited, GPO Box 1203, Sydney NSW 1045.
This edition published 2001 for INDEX: Henson Way, Kettering, NN16 8PX, United Kingdom
Reprinted 2001 in Singapore by Tien Wah Press.
ISBN: 1 89773 062 4
First printed 1994. Reprinted 1995, 1996, 1998, 1999, 2000, 2001. Printed in Hong Kong by Toppan Printing.

Managing Editor: Rachel Carter. **Food Editors:** Kerrie Ray, Tracy Rutherford. **Editor:** Amanda Bishop. **Designer:** Wing Ping Tong. **Recipe Development:** Tracy Rutherford, Tracey Port, Jacki Passmore, Jenny Grainger. **Food Stylist:** Carolyn Fienberg, Mary Harris. **Photographers:** Luis Martin, Andrew Furlong, Reg Morrison (Steps). **Food Preparation:** Jo Forrest, Tracey Port, Melanie McDermott.
CEO & Publisher: Anne Wilson.
National Library of Australia Cataloguing-in-Publication Data. Sensational barbecues step-by-step. Includes index. Barbecue cookery. 641.82.

Front cover: Curly Endive Salad (page 80), and a selection of delicious barbecued food from the book.
Inside front cover: Chicken Breasts with Fruit Medley (top) and Tandoori Chicken Skewers (both page 57).